Abraham Perry Miller

Consolation and other Poems

Abraham Perry Miller

Consolation and other Poems

ISBN/EAN: 9783744710343

Printed in Europe, USA, Canada, Australia, Japan

Cover: Foto ©Thomas Meinert / pixelio.de

More available books at **www.hansebooks.com**

AND

OTHER POEMS,

BY

ABRAHAM PERRY MILLER.

———

NEW YORK:

BRENTANO BROS.

1886.

CONTENTS.

CONTENTS.

PREFACE.

Poetry is its own excuse for being,
And Poems are begotten and not made,
Being of one substance with the Poet's soul;
The living germs, dowered with perpetual life,
Are in the mind, till vivifying Love,
Clasping the Poet in divine embrace,
Draws forth the spark of an immortal song,
Which, fed and cultured, grows to its own sphere,
Like a developed and harmonious spirit,
A glory and a comfort to the world !

Suggestion is the law of Poetry.
Poetry is the spirit's lightning, which reveals,
By vivid flashes of electric thought,
That dread, divine gratuity named Life:
Fathomless yearnings, mysteries infinite,
Self wars, soul triumphs, white-hot agonies,
As lightning bursts reveal the infinite night,
Fathomless skies of cloud, vast scopes of earth,
Wide sea expanses, looming mountain heights,
Deep yawning gulfs, and rivers, plains and woods.

Poetry is the language of the skies;
The Heavens commune in musical discourse;
All lives must live to music or must perish;
The law of deathless life is harmony.

The Poet's pen is the enchanter's wand,
The Ithuriel spear, the sceptre of the king,
The master's baton and the painter's brush,
Tripod and trident and diviner's rod;
All arts in one; whatever is, is his.

Dear Children of the Heart! go forth and meet
Bravely your fate in a discordant world.
We love our own, ill-favored though they seem
To those who cannot love them.   Issue forth
And live your sweet lives gladly, doubting not
That many hearts will love you.   'Tis the fate
Of all immortal things to be beloved.

CONSOLATION.

I.

PRELUDE.

My Poet-Friend, to-night thy Soul is near,
I know thy sorrow, and it makes thee dear;
And never yet was man or woman born,
Who did not some time offer love for scorn.

I have been out around the dear old town,
Long walking to and fro, and up and down,
About the much-loved streets and flowery ways,
Where, soul to soul, we walked in other days,
And now returned, with Brain and Soul on fire,
Filled with immortal yearning and desire,
I write my thoughts and send them unto thee,
Across the Mountains to the distant Sea !

To-night, O Friend ! I feel the old unrest,
The strain, and stir, and tumult in the breast,
As though the Soul assailed its walls of clay
On every side, and strove to break away !
So have I seen a Lion in his cage
Spring at the iron bars in helpless rage,

Or plunge against the walls with fruitless bound,
And with loud protests shake the buildings round !
To-night there comes the longing to be free,
Away beyond the Mountains and the Sea—
Away through skies to some more glorious clime,
From the poor Present to some richer Time—
Away, away forever ! Ah, how vain !
For are they Free who break this mortal chain ?
Flies in the cobweb of relentless Fate,
Our struggling souls resent the present state;
Each soul a Tantalus, and over each
Forever hangs the Bliss it cannot reach !

I know thy grief, and yet how shall I write ?
To comfort thee, what shall I say to-night ?
That thou art not alone ?   Behold the throng
Of wounded souls that bear some gloomy wrong.
Ah, sorrowing friend ! what multitudes to-day
Walk by thy side, unknown, the thorny way,
And walk in darkness, praying for the light,
Like one who walks his chamber in the night,
And ever through the windows looks away
Into the chilly night, and longs for day !

There is no soul but has some dear regret
For something lost on which the heart was set;
Through tear-drop prisms still we see it glow,
Rimmed with the splendors of the glorious bow.
There is no soul but sometimes takes its flight
To those far skies that made its youth so bright,
In search of something lost, and, with a sigh,

Gives o'er the search, returns, and waits to die,
And treads the stony way with bleeding feet,
To find it when the heart has ceased to beat.

Now that thy love is spurned and undertrod,
Fly thou to Nature, Poetry and God;
Nay, fly to Love itself, and Love shall be
Its own strong healer, and shall set thee free.

II.

NATURE.

How sweet to know in all the wounds we feel,
The mystic power that Nature has to heal,
The strength and comfort found by him who flies
From human contests to the fields and skies—
The blest escape from conflict and from care,
As though the God of Comfort met us there !

I have not soared to God to walk with Him,
And my rapt visions have been brief and dim,
Although, like Paul, I fought against the flesh,
With every power, and prayer, and thought, and wish,
Yet when abroad with Nature, ranging free,
God met me on the hills, and walked with me !
O sweet Autumnal days of long ago !
How in my bosom yet their raptures glow !
Those mellow days, when in the infinite West,
In some celestial island of the blest,
The Angels loosed the winds and set them free,
To roam the fields and woods and hills with me,

While toiling men, in hamlets far away,
Heard the woods roar through all the balmy day.

O blessed days of sunshine and of peace !
When from the strife of men I stole release,
And walked abroad among the hills and woods,
In the sweet company of God's solitudes;
Through velvet fields I saw the rivers run,
And white towns shining in the mellow sun,
And heard the woods their soothing music pour
From forest harps with multitudinous roar;
Or saw, across some blue and distant bay,
A glory fall on cities far away,
And taper steeples, tow'ring slim and high,
Stand glorified against th' ineffable sky !
And then God came with His rich gifts of power,
And talked and walked with me from hour to hour,
And changed me to a Harp of living chords,
From which He drew such strains as Heaven affords;
Nor could I yield when sheltered safe and warm
And Night shut down around me with a Storm,
For still, above the darkness and the rain,
My Soul went out to walk with God again !

And years have passed, and yet, with many a thrill,
The old, old love of Nature sways me still !
And down the great deeps of the throbbing soul,
To-night what sounds and waves of rapture roll,
As thunder-balls, from some Olympus hurled,
Roll down the sky and shake the solid world !

This Summer Night is neither cool nor warm,
But fresh and fragrant from the blessed storm,
Which, still receding through the glorious night,
Lights up the sky with endless sheets of light,
Shot up, divergent, from the realms below,
Followed by hoarse and sullen booms, as though
Some Planet had exploded and uphurled
The splendid ruins through the upper world !

All through the afternoon the dreamy day
Swam listless o'er the Earth, and far away
The lazy clouds went loitering round the sky,
Or sat far up and dozed on mountains high.
The green trees drooped, the panting cattle lay
In the warm shade and fought the flies away.
Along the world's far verge and down the sky,
Cloud Panoramas loomed and glided by,
Rocks, icebergs, mountains, capped with luminous
  snow,
And hundred-towered cities, moving slow !
And then, with banners round the West unfurled,
The great red Sun went down behind the world,
And, eastward, looming o'er the hills, Night's rim,
Like a World's Ghost, rose ill-defined and dim !

Around the West, in many a purple fold,
The delicate-textured clouds lay fringed with gold,
As though the gods had thrown their cloaks aside,
For some high pastime played at eventide;
And where the sun went down the glowing sky
Was all on fire; intense and flaming high,

The light burned upward, like some furnace vast,
Where Heaven's ore is into planets cast,
And then sent forth, each world to take its place,
And spin for cycles through the realms of space !
Then when the fire burned down, across the West
A Thunder-Storm upheaved its golden crest,
Alive with lightning, that, with wondrous freaks,
Played o'er the cloud-built cliffs and mountain peaks,
As though the gods, on some great work intent,
Into the sky had heaved a Continent !

And now, while yet above the sky was blue,
And all God's worlds came thronging into view,
From out the West there came a cooling breeze,
Which went about and whispered to the trees
That o'er the mountains and the western plain,
Sweeping this way, there was a mighty rain !
And we, who sat beneath, the whispering heard,
And knew its meaning clear as human word.
Then all the glad trees, with the news elate,
Waved leaves and branches with commotion great,
As men hear good news of some great affair
And wave their hats and handkerchiefs in air !

Anon the storm came on.   The lightning fell
In seas of fire upon every hill !
The crashing thunder split th' eternal walls,
And rumbled down the sky like rolling balls,
And gathered all its strength and burst again,
And shook the world from mountain-top to plain !
And all the woods and echoing mountains round,

And all the hills and vales and quiv'ring ground,
And all the hollow sky, and every cloud,
Filled with the thunder, bellowed long and loud !
Down came the rain, as though the streams on high
Had burst their banks and overflowed the sky !
And sweeping on with mighty rush and beat
And roar and tramp of multitudinous feet,
Washed off the world and left it fresh and sweet !

Then passed the storm, and left us such a night
As only storms can leave us in their flight !
So bland the air, that all the sounds seem near,
And turn to music on the quickened ear;
Even from the hillsides out beyond the town,
The shouts and laughter come distinctly down.
Beyond the hills huge piles of cloud are blown,
And round the heavens in mountainous masses strown,
For miles and miles the cloudy ruins lie,
Like broken hills and mountains in the sky,
As though an earthquake, reaching from below,
Had crushed a world to pieces at a blow !
And clear above me, rising free and high,
Sweeps the vast wonder of the endless sky,
Sprinkled with flying worlds that, in their flight,
Shine, like good men, to give each other light !
Thus, in the busy day, one world alone
Of all the million million worlds is shown;
But in the night, when men have time to gaze,
God draws the curtain, and His Heaven displays !
Far off a light shoots down the azure wall,
(As though an Angel let a star-lamp fall !)

While the great starry highway built through space,
Runs off to some remote and happy place—
Runs up, perchance, to God's own bright abode
In the sky's centre ! for so rich is God,
He builds the very highway to His throne,
Of worlds more grand and costly than our own !

Enough ! enough ! Yet I could dwell all night,
With never-weary and supreme delight,
On Nature's beauty and the joys that stir
The souls of those who give their love to her !

III.

SONG.

Ah, bitterest cup of all ! that thy rich power,
Thy gift of Song, thy more than regal dower—
Which wins thee Fame and should have won thee Love—
That this itself thy grief and shame should prove !
How didst thou look to this high gift of Song,
To win thee triumph over every wrong,
While in thy heart forever rose the thought
That this high power would bring thee love unsought.
O misplaced love ! Her heart, unskilled and hard,
O'erlooked the Man because she scorned the Bard !

And now, beloved friend, whate'er betide,
I do entreat thee not to turn aside,
For when great gifts or deeds bring grief and shame,
Heaven pays us back in wealth of love and fame !
Whate'er befall, be true to thy own heart,

Nor from thy Poet-Purpose once depart;
And gain, like Bards of old, the power divine
To put a life's quintessence in a line !

O grand old Bards ! whose fine-knit souls at birth
Were dipped in beauty ! How they walked the earth,
Big with rich thought and bursting to express !
And spake to music those high thoughts which bless.
In words that strike like lightning, (being stung
Or touched by outrage), from a fire-tipt tongue,
Satire and deathless song broke forth alive,
Like bees and honey from a broken hive !
What grip of brain ! what telescopic eye !
To range for lofty thoughts through earth and sky,
To hold and warm and shape them in the mind
Into eternal life, to bless mankind !

There is no power like the power to sing;
Be thou a Poet rather than a King !
Nor let this disappointment for one hour
Turn thee aside to grasp at wealth or power.
Stoop not at all, nor ape a worldling life,
In hope to win a worldling for a wife;
These ask the Eagle, made for lofty flight,
Likewise to be an Owl and hoot at night.
Shun the whole brood, whate'er their rank or place,
Who turn toward the world a smiling face,
While in their charnel hearts, that lie behind,
Dwell evil thoughts and lusts of every kind.
Like jails that show a fair front to the street,

With yards thick-set with shrubs and flowers sweet,
While just behind, in many a stony cell,
Barred by iron grates, the thieves and murd'rers dwell !

Cling to thy Muse, and her strong wings shall bear
Thy wounded heart above this brief despair.
O precious gift of Song ! how Bards have found
In their own lays a balm for every wound :

How glows the heart to read of Olney's Bard,
With fate at once so tender and so hard,
Who fled the tumult of the mad'ning throng,
And led a life more precious than his song—
Who made the Muse a refuge in despair,
And to the ages laid his spirit bare !
Men called him mad, yet there has lived no man
More sane in spirit since the world began.
How wise in lowly and in lofty things !
What other harp so full of holy strings !
His misnamed madness was the Spirit's way
To tune the lyre for an immortal lay !

Arch-Poet Milton, when his sight was gone,
And age, ill-health and penury came on,
When friends fell off and round him densely rose,
In Church and State, his strong, triumphant foes,
Dropped the iron pen that on the nations broke
And conquered Europe by its mighty stroke,
And gave his soul to those divine delights
Which Poets know who scale celestial heights—

Turned his grand face from all his bitter foes,
And o'er his age to endless glory rose !

O Bard divine ! who from his blooming youth,
Kept himself true to Beauty and to Truth—
Kept himself free from every vice and crime,
Therefore God filled his soul with thoughts sublime,
And lit within his breast that seraph flame
Which filled the earth and heavens with his fame !

IV.

LOVE.

How shall I speak of that which dealt the blow ?
That source of all thy shame and all thy woe ?
Yet Love itself shall be the cure of Love,
And heal all wounds in earth and heaven above.
Keep faith in Love, the cure of every curse—
The strange, sweet wonder of the universe !
God loves a lover, and, while time shall roll,
This wonder, Love, shall save the human soul !
Love is the heart's condition; grave or gay,
And youth or age, alike must own its sway.
Age crowns the head with venerable snow,
But Life and Love forever mated go;
Along life's far frontier the aged move,
One foot beyond, and nothing left but Love,
And when the Soul its mortal part resigns,
The perfect world of Love around it shines !

O beauteous dream ! the early dream of Love !
When Heaven runs, through channels from above,
An undercurrent through the blooming heart !
O gray-beard men amid the busy mart,
How would ye give all gain ye ever knew
To wake and find Youth's dream of love come true !
O early Love ! far-streaming up life's height,
And tinging it with gold and purple light,
As when, at dawn, before the coming sun,
Far up the sky the hues of morning run !
O riper Love ! that gives a rosy hue
To all men suffer and to all they do !
Thou one true joy! or when or where thou art,
Strength, inspiration, bliss of every heart !

O sweet old story ! told ten thousand times
In honied prose and in delicious rhymes,
Forever old and yet forever new,
A Fairy Tale forever coming true !

My splendid friend ! I see a coming day,
When from thy heart this cloud shall float away—
When thou shalt pass far up the shining height,
Thy forehead bathed in Fame's eternal light,
And at thy side shall walk the blessed wife
Whom Heaven shall send to hallow thy pure life,
To sweeten every cup which Fate supplies,
And give new beauty to the earth and skies;
Thy Counterpart, with tender hands endowed,
To smooth thy brow and brush away the cloud,
Be Mother, Sister, Friend, Companion, Wife,
And in a sunrise glory bathe thy life !

v.

RELIGION.

One other source remains to soothe thy breast,
The one Great Comfort which includes the rest:
Submit thy Sorrow and thy Soul to God,
And learn what peace it is to kiss His rod,
Who answers Wishes ere they turn to Prayers,
And with His Blessing takes us unawares—
Who girds us, though we know Him not, and stands
Above us always with His helping hands.
As when a little child, returned from play,
Finds the door closed and latched across its way,
Against the door, with infant push and strain,
It gathers all its strength and strives in vain;
Unseen within a loving father stands
And lifts the iron latch with easy hands;
Then, as he lightly draws the door aside,
He hides behind it, while, with baby pride,
And face aglow, in struts the little one,
Flushed and rejoiced to think what it has done !
So when men find, across life's rugged way,
Strong doors of Trouble barred from day to day,
And strive with all their power of knees and hands,
Unseen within their Heavenly Father stands,
And lifts each iron latch, while men pass through,
Flushed and rejoiced to think what they can do !

Turn to the Helper, unto whom thou art
More near and dear than to thy mother's heart,
Who is more near to thee than is the blood

That warms thy bosom with its purple flood—
Who, by a word, can change the mental state,
And make a burden light, however great !

O Loving Power! that, dwelling deep within,
Consoles our spirits in their woe and sin:
When days were dark and all the world went wrong,
Nor any heart was left for prayer or song—
When bitter Memory, o'er and o'er again,
Revolved the wrongs endured from fellow-men,
And told how hopes decayed and bore no fruit,
And He who placed us here was deaf and mute!
If then we turned on God in angry wise,
And scanned his dealings with reproachful eyes,
Questioned His goodness, and, in foolish wrath,
Called Hope a lie and ridiculed our Faith,
Did we not find, in such an evil hour,
That far within us dwelt this Loving Power?
No wrathful God without to smite us down,
Or turn His face away with angry frown;
But in the bitter heart a smile began,
Grew, all at once, within, and upward ran,
Broke out upon the face, and, for a while,
Despite all bitterness, we had to smile!
Because God's Spirit that within us lay,
Simply rose up and smiled our wrath away!

This love endures through all things, without end,
And every soul has one Almighty Friend,
Whose Angels watch and tend it from its birth,
And Heaven becomes the servant of the Earth!

Whate'er befall, our spirits live and move
In one vast ocean of Eternal Love!
Sink where we may, we sink into the skies,
Touch God in sinking, and begin to rise!

O wondrous race! this human race of ours,
So small in space! so limited in powers!
And yet so formed that all the gods above   .
Are drawn toward us by 'resistless love!
Man is so fashioned that his faintest sigh
Draws down a god to help him from the sky!
Fav'rite of Heaven! whom Angels strive to please!
Borne in their arms and dandled on their knees!
Creation's Baby! blest amid the Curse!
The Pet and Darling of the universe!

" Ah, beauteous faith! my friend," I hear thee say,
" But who shall take this bitter cup away?"
He who prepared it.   When thy quiv'ring soul
Has drained it dry, this cup may make thee whole.
Our hearts are eggs, and God must break the shell
To get the treasure which He loves so well.

I·hold these sorrows of the human heart
As God's supreme and never-failing art
To round us into Angels, and to warm
Our throbbing souls to some diviner form!
As on some Summer night along the sky,
A mountain-range of cloud moves slowly by,
Now looming dark, and now with fire ablaze,
As o'er the floating mass the lightning plays;

So moves the soul of man, now dark, now bright,
And so God plays upon it with His light!

Yes, beauteous faith, indeed, a faith I draw
From Human Reason and Eternal Law,
And not from man-made creeds of long ago,
Contrived by men whose minds were crude and low.

O loving God of Nature! who through all,
Has never yet betrayed me to a fall,
While, following creeds of men, I went astray,
And in distressing mazes lost my way;
But turning back to Thee, I found Thee true,
And sweet as woman's love and fresh as dew!
Henceforth on Thee, and Thee alone, I rest,
Nor warring sects shall tear me from Thy breast.
While others doubt and wrangle o'er their creeds,
I rest in Thee and satisfy my needs.

As some huge mountain crowned with waving pines,
When Winter rages or when Summer shines,
Still lifts its head unchanging and serene,
Forever rooted and forever green;
Though on its head the furious tempests beat,
And whelming torrents thunder round its feet!
From every winter and from every storm
It still comes forth more beautiful in form,
And while with unmoved feet on earth it stands,
Amid the sky its peaceful brow expands;
So stands the man whose spirit rests upon
That Rock of Ages, the Eternal One!

When Winter rages, still his leaves are green;
When tempests beat, his soul remains serene;
Whatever wars assail or thunders roll,
They only round and beautify his soul!
And, raised above the strife that round him lies,
He stands on earth with head amid the skies!

But seek Him not in human creeds and shrines,
When through all Nature everywhere He shines,
When in thy soul He dwells to answer thee,
To prompt and warn, to guide and make thee free.

Dear Friend, I know how in our happier days,
Thy generous spirit longed for love and praise;
Both shall be thine, for great thy fame must be,
If thou wilt use the gift God gave to thee.
But far above all search for human Fame
There lies a nobler and diviner aim,
And to do good is more than to have won
All Fame that can be won beneath the sun.

What hosts whose power and fame on earth are vast,
Shall wake beyond obscure and weak at last,
To find their deeds have never borne their fame
Above the lower plane from which they came !
While toiling millions who are meek and poor,
Whose lives are humble and whose names obscure,
Shall find their deeds have borne their fame away
To Summer lands that bask in endless day!
Poor and unknown they shall lie down and die,
But wake up rich and famous in the sky,

Pleased and surprised to find their names are known
Through the bright realms around the Great White
  Throne!

As once I sang, again I sing to-night
Of that incoming Day whose purer light
Already fills the sky.   Even now the sun
Of the New Age is up and day begun:

Roll on, O slow-wheeled Years! and bring the day
When men shall gather wealth to give away;
And spring to help when tempted nature falls,
As when a builder drops from city walls;
When to do good alone men shall be bold,
And seek out Suffering as they seek for Gold;
When Christian women shall not wipe their feet
Upon their fallen sisters in the street;
And Calumny shall be a crime unknown,
And each shall make his neighbor's wrong his own!

Be gone! O Hate and Wrong and War, be gone!
Roll on this way, O Golden Age! roll on!
When Men and Angels face to face shall talk,
And Earth and Heaven arm in arm shall walk—
When Love shall reign, and over sea and shore
The Peace of God shall rest for evermore!

Good night, my Poet-Friend! with soul on fire,
Filled with immortal yearning and desire,
I write my thoughts and send them unto thee,
Across the mountains to the distant sea!

THE GHOST.

OR POE'S " RAVEN " REVERSED.

Once at night, while sitting lonely in my chamber, thinking only
  Of a saintly maid who left me in the happy days of yore,
In the air I heard a snapping, and upon the walls a rapping,
  Like the dripping, dropping, tapping, of the rain-drops on the floor—
  Heard a measured, muffled dropping, as of water on the floor—
      Heard but this, and nothing more.

Presently the sounds drew nearer, and the drop, drop, drop grew clearer,
  And I started from my reverie this mystery to explore,
While I said: " 'Tis only fancy, yet a weirdness in it daunts me,
  "And perchance some Spirit haunts me, coming from some ghostly shore,
  " Yet no ghost from out that realm ever came to me before,—
     " 'Tis caprice, and nothing more."

While I doubted thus, uncertain, Something rustled
    like a curtain,
  Or a woman's silken garment touching on the cush-
    ioned floor,
And I felt a cold wind blowing, like the chill night air
    inflowing,
  The weird source of which not knowing, I then
    cried, in wonder sore:
  "Is this Fancy, Fear, or Phantom come from out
    some ghostly shore ?
      "Is this whim, or something more ?"

Then a sense of Some One present, and a thrill, in-
    tense, but pleasant,
  Broke in waves upon my spirit, like the waves upon
    the shore;
And a nameless terror filled me, as through every vein
    it chilled me,
  And with pain and pleasure thrilled me—thrilled me
    to my being's core !
  And I said: " This strange experience is no Fancy, I
    am sure—
      "This is surely something more !"

Still my questioning could summon no response from
    man or woman,
  And the stillness now grew dreadful as the thun-
    der's peal and roar,
While the air around grew yellow, from a radiant ghost-
    ly halo,

And a jasmine fragrance mellow to my quickened
    nostrils bore,
And an opalescent disk, or spot, appeared upon the
    floor,
        Moving, rising more and more !

Whence a luminous mist or vapor, shaped and shin-
    ing like a taper,
Rose upon the air beside me and the carpet floated
    o'er;
And this radiant Apparition opened like a flower Ely-
    sian,
And I saw the loveliest Vision ever mortal saw be-
    fore—
For there stood the fairest Ghost that ever stood by
    man before—
        Stood and smiled, and nothing more !

Fashioned like a maiden slender, and with luminous
    eyes, and tender,
This fair Ghost looked out upon me with a love
    divine and pure.
"Comest thou," I said, "to charm me? for I know
    thou canst not harm me;
  "Who and whence art thou, inform me?—Phantom
    from some heavenly shore !"
Then this Vision, or this virgin visitor, from some
    immortal shore,
        Whispered, "Thine Forevermore !"

Speechless, then, I sat and pondered, while within my
    heart I wondered
  Whether this were one who left me in the days that
    are no more—
Whether this could be the maiden who, when Earth
    was all an Eden,
  Which we roamed, and loved, and played in, quit
    my side and went before?
And she knew my thought, and answered, "I am
    she that went before,
         "And am Thine Forevermore!"

"Spirit," said I, "maid immortal! sent this night
    through Heaven's portal,
  "Tell me, is our love eternal?" "Yes," she said,
    "forever sure,
"And it cannot swerve or vary, for I am thy True
    Love, Mary,
  "And, though seeming light and airy, I am real, as
    of yore;
  "And thy spirit ever draws me—I am with thee ever-
    more—
        "Thou art Mine Forevermore!"

Suddenly, with transport gifted, into rapturous rapport
    lifted,
  With her glorious spirit-womanhood forever young
    and pure,
"Angel!" cried I, "do not leave me—sure, no Angel
    could deceive me—

"Stay until I can believe thee and my doubting
　soul assure !"
Then she breathed upon me softly and she answered
　as before—
　　　"Thou art Mine Forevermore !"

"Can no fate this union sever ?" said I.　And she an-
　swered: "Never !—
"Not till God and thou and Angels will our love
　to be no more;
"For True Marriage is eternal, and True Love for-
　ever vernal,
　"And each soul in spheres supernal shall its own
　　True Mate secure.
　"We are Counterparts eternal and must love for-
　　evermore—
　　　"We are One Forevermore !"

"Warp and woof we are inwoven, and our Dual-Soul,
　uncloven,
　"In the Heavens shall be One Angel to aspire and
　　adore;
"And if, in thy dark despairing, thou couldst see thy
　Home preparing
　"By our spirit-love and caring, thou wouldst know
　　despair no more;
　"And thy feet shall touch the table-lands before
　　earth-life is o'er,
　　　"And shall weary Nevermore !"

"Spirit," said I, "I am weary, and my life is lone and
dreary,

"And, if Heaven has given thee power, take me
with thee, I implore !"

"Rest must come by Heaven's bestowing," said she,
"but, when Self foregoing,

"And by holy deeds outflowing, thou canst do the
service pure

"Which the Angel-World assigns thee, thou shalt
join me on this shore,

"And be with me Evermore !"

Seeing then my disappointment, she out-poured this
spirit ointment:—

"Let this promise be thy guiding-star till earthly life
is o'er—

"That I love and cannot grieve thee, and I never can
deceive thee,

"I will never, never leave thee, and will help thee
to endure;

"All that mortal love can do for thee, that will I
do, and more,

"I will help thee Evermore !"

"Angel !" said I, "Ghost or Woman ! nothing so
divinely human,

"Or so womanly and wifely, ever came to me before !"

"Love," she said, "this hour is glorious, and my mission is victorious,

" Now no power can ever lure us from our blessed
    love of yore;
" This communion is the way to Heaven, and Hea-
    ven's very door—
      " Love is Heaven Forevermore !"

" Shall our life be calm enjoyment? shall there not be
    high employment
  " For our fond and fervid spirits when we meet to
    part no more?"
" Yes," she said, " mankind are brothers, and our
    bliss is in another's—
  " When we make a Heaven for others, our own
    Heaven we secure;
  " Even in Heaven life is effort, but our strife is high
    and pure—
      " Life is effort Evermore."

" Guardian, guide and bride forever," said I, " why did
    Heaven dissever
  " Our young lives on Earth and doom me to a fate
    so lone and poor?"
" Love," she said, " the immortal Powers knew that
    souls endued like ours
  " Blossom best to perfect flowers when the one is
    gone before:
  " Thus our spirits grow to harmony and love which
    shall endure,
      " Ever pure and Evermore !"

Then a sense of her devotion thrilled my soul with
    deep emotion,
  And I said, "What worthy recompense can mortal
    man restore?"
"Love," she said, "'tis mutual giving, each upon the
    other living;
  "I am spirit-food receiving when thy thoughts are
    high and pure;
  "Thus the two worlds on each other, in one destiny
    secure,
        "Are dependent Evermore!"

Touched she then my forehead faintly, with her vestal
    lips and saintly,
  In a holy kiss that thrilled me to my spirit's very
    core,
And she said, "The strength sustaining this revealment
    fast is waning,
  "There is but a breath remaining till our interview is
    o'er,
  "But remember I am with thee, and I love thee
    evermore—
        "Only Love Forevermore!"

Then she passed into the vapor shaped and shining
    like a taper,
  Shedding o'er my soul an influence which shall last
    forevermore;
And this Maiden-Angel lowly, bright and beautiful
    and holy,

Left a glory where she slowly, slowly melted to the
   floor,—
Left a halo and a glory shining there upon the floor—
   Shining there Forevermore !

And that Glory, undeclining, is forever shining, shining,
   With a light above the sunlight there upon my chamber floor;
And that Light my soul is saving—in that Light my
   soul is laving—
   All the ills of Time out-braving till I meet her on
   that shore,
   And my soul into that Heaven which is imaged
   on the floor,
      Shall be lifted Evermore !

THE NEW ANNUS MIRABILIS.

THE YEAR OF FAMINE AND FIRE.

In that far orient realm where the gales,
Faint with their loads of perfume from the vales,
That Land of Roses, long by poets sung,
Whose tales of love are told in every tongue;
The gaunt-faced Famine walks abroad to smite,
Like one who smote the Assyrian host at night.
In all the lovely realms round Ispahan,
The people throng the towns with faces wan,
And faint and fall in fruitless search for bread,
And fill the streets and highways with the dead.
The very flowers that in the valleys blow,
Die on their stems amid the general woe,
And those who only knew to scent the rose,
Now scent the dead in every breeze that blows!

Nor yet the Old World feels the rod alone,
Above the giant New a great light shone—
Shone like the Aurora on some winter night,
And half the world beheld the lurid light.
On woods and towns a fiery tempest beat,
And woods and towns dissolved with fervent heat,
As though a snow-storm swept along the lakes,
With flame for winds and red-hot coals for flakes,

Or Heaven had sent an Angel in its ire,
And set the very winds and clouds on fire!
Men, fleeing to the streams and lakes to save,
Leaped from a fiery to a watery grave,
Some plunged down wells headlong in their despair!
The Fire pursued them down and killed them there;
One slew his children in the mad desire
To save them from the cruel death by fire;
One heard the roar and hitched his team and fled,
With wife and little ones just snatched from bed;
The flames reached up behind with daggers red,
And left him mad and fleeing with his dead!
Ten score of men, by vengeful flames pursued,
Fled to one house that isolated stood;
The flames surround them like a troop from hell,
And touched to crisp by fiery spears they fell!
And when the storm of fire had passed away,
A thousand dead in fields and cities lay!

While to and fro went forth the Fiery Power,
Like Satan, seeking whom it might devour;
It came one night, that closed a day of rest,
To that precocious city of the West;
That wonder which, by some Enchanter's Wand,
Rose a great city out of mud and sand;
Sprang forward like a steed and came abreast,
And passed and led the cities of the West.
As though in some remote and Western wild,
A settler's cabin-born and lusty child,
Should spring to vigorous manhood in an hour,
And lead the greatest in the race for power!

Fair lay the city on that Sabbath night,
With many a lofty spire and flaring light,
The maiden slept with white hands on her breast,
The mother laid her little ones to rest,
The lovers kissed by many a cosy fire,
The poor man dreamed and had his heart's desire,
The rich men smiled in many a palace home,
And thought of all the wealth and power to come,
The watchmen in the streets strode up and down,
Vain of their power to keep the sleeping town.

The Fire looked down on all the happy scene,
The rows of blocks with lighted streets between,
And then, descending on the town, became,
In a dark place, a little torch of flame;
Then, spreading right and left, it grew and grew,
Exulting in the deed it came to do!
Steady at first from house to house it stept,
Then took the wind, and like a tempest swept.
On! on! it sweeps toward the heart of town;
Street after street of massive blocks go down!
The very stone walls burst to sheets of flame,
And wood and iron buildings burn the same!
Sometimes with greedy haste it runs unseen.
Along the street and leaves a space between;
Enters some building at a secret place—
At every window shows its horrid face,
And reaching forth a thousand hands of flame,
And all around, and back the way it came,
Fires all the blocks and melts the towering walls,

And leaps exulting as each structure falls!
The very River fails its march to stay;
It leaps across and still pursues its way!
Melts down like lead, the blocks of costly piles,
And flames and rages through the town for miles!
And now it turns to streets it left behind,
And beats back spitefully against the wind;
Flies in the rough face of the furious blast,
And grasps the palace homes and holds them fast;
Holds fast the rich men's homes, nor lets them go, ·
Till, leveled with the rest, it lays them low!
Thus through the lurid night and awful day,
Against the helpless town it had its way;
And when it paused to count its trophies o'er,
The ruined structures summed a thousand score!

While thus the fire on things insensate wrought,
Men fought at first, but knew in vain they fought,
Themselves attacked, they quit the hopeless strife,
And flee through all the flaming streets for life;
Some quit the fiery land and refuge take,
Amid the quenching waters of the lake;
The vengeful Fire that cannot pass the land,
Strives all the day to reach them where they stand,
And keeps them in the waves and strikes at them,
With long white arms of hot and spiteful flame !
Some died in rooms amid the roaring hell,
Some, on the streets surrounded, gasped and fell,
And men and beasts by frantic thousands came,
Scourged through the scorching streets with whips of
        flame!

To open fields and parks beyond the town,
Where, like the scattered flocks, they laid them down,
A hundred thousand souls from shelter driven—
Their bed the ground, their roof the stormy heaven;
And there from icy cold and sore affright,
The feeble perished in the open night!

And now the Pucks, unknown to our sires,
That girdle earth along the slender wires,
Took their slim paths that stretched on every hand,
And spread the cry of " Fire !" through the land !
In all the startled towns the people ran,
Succor to send and quick relief to plan!
Men, women, children, gave their hard-earned store,
And hands reached forth to help from every door!
Before the sun went down and closed the day,
Long thundering trains were sweeping on their way,
Breaking with loads of raiment and of food,
To save the stripped and hungry multitude!
Men ran to all the stations with their store,
And chid because the trains could bear no more,
Pursued the fleeing cars across the plains,
And threw their offerings on the bursting trains.
'Twas not one City's, but the Nation's fire,
Nay, Europe's self, along the ocean wire,
Reached up a hand to save, nor reached alone,
The whole world joined and made the fire its own;
And men rejoiced that, o'er the strife and din,
A great distress could make the whole world kin!

Thus fell Chicago! but above the plain
A greater city she shall rise again,
Cleansed by the Fire from germs of foul decay,
And moral plagues and follies burned away.
As when the fire fell on London town,
And raged for days, and smote the city down,
It burned the dens where pestilence was bred,
And caught the Plague itself and struck it dead!
In mercy sent, it burned the curse away,
And cleansed the city to this very day!

MINNESOTA.

————

READ AT THE CELEBRATION OF THE 200TH ANNIVER-
SARY OF THE DISCOVERY OF ST. ANTHONY FALLS,
MINNEAPOLIS, JULY 3, 1880.

————

Down these great rocks the mighty river poured,
And like an endless tempest beat and roared,
Ages on ages of uncounted years,
Before its thunder fell on human ears;
In one great song that made the woods rejoice,
Praising its Maker with a ceaseless voice !
Then the Mound Builders came, with awkward toil,
And built their mounds and tilled the barbarous soil,
Yoked the wild bison to some uncouth plow,
And cleft the rivers with a birchen prow.
Then came the Red Man, stoical and brave,
Of whom no power on earth can make a slave,
True to the true, and good toward the good,
And, like his Christian brother, spilling blood.
Human as we, whate'er his savage arts,
For veins of gold run through his heart of quartz !
Here round the Falls he built his rude tepee,
Made love and danced and fought and died as we.
And centuries went by, and then there came,
For love of Mother Church and France and Fame,
The man who gave the Falls their saintly name.

O Priests! destined to pierce the wilderness,
Yours to explore and ours to possess,
Yours to uplift the cross by every stream,
And ours to build and realize your dream!

Anon the Saxon came, whose iron hand,
Has one strong finger laid on every land,
Who through his loom runs all the threads of race,
And leaves a grander Saxon in his place.

The doughty Dutchman from his dykes escaped,
With wives and ships to one plump model shaped,
Spreads round the Hudson in phlegmatic ease,
And smokes his pipe and trades to every breeze;
The gifted Frenchman, panting to be free,
And smit with love of fame and liberty,
Kisses Columbia on her river mouth,
And builds his New World Paris in the south;
The swarthy Spaniard plants his homes and vines
Where down the coast the yellow metal shines,
And counts his beads and tells his herds and flocks,
Till at his door the sturdy Saxon knocks;
But build where'er they may, they build in vain,
The land is not for Holland, France nor Spain;
The all-absorbing Saxon, East or West,
Like Aaron's serpent-rod, devours the rest;
His tongue and faith, his name and laws, he leaves
On every soil his conq'ring plow-share cleaves.

Yet, blood-stained Saxon! storming round the
world
With battle-ax, and bloody flag unfurled,

Cleaving the skull of every weaker race,
Shall not God's lightning smite you on the face?
Beware! for though the Red man finds no God
To keep his waning race above the sod,
Yet every wrong to white or black or red,
Falls back at last upon the culprit's head.
For every Black Man killed in Slavery's name,
Two White Men perished when the crisis came,
And twice the wealth amassed by unpaid toil,
Went down in war's grim waste and debt and spoil!
And is the Red Man, though foredoomed to fall,
Less dear to Him who made and loves us all?

Now came the time, (so near it seems to stand
That one might almost reach it with his hand,)
When the great human tide rolled up the strand,
And bird and beast and savage fled the land!
And lo! the infant Lowell of the West,
Lay like a Fondling on the prairie's breast!

To-day the child, to stalwart manhood grown,
Has won a name that round the world is known!
I see the tow'ring stack that cleaves the air,
The pond'rous engine-stroke, the furnace-glare,
And hear the roar of trade, the whirr of wheels,
The buzz of saws, the hum of giant mills.
On every wind is heard the signal scream
Of iron chariots made alive by steam,
While, like great shuttles, flashing to and fro,
And ever in and out, they come and go,

As in this warp they weave the woof of wealth,
And through our commerce pour the blood of health.
Forth from this mart, through empires near and far,
Flies the iron chariot and the thund'ring car,
Like some great Dragon from the Furies hurled,
Yoked to a Juggernaut to crush the world !
Fleet as the arrow from the Red Man's bow,
Down through the vales and up the steeps they go,
Dive through the hills, and, bursting forth again,
Shout to the busy towns and shake the plain !

Fit place to meet ! fit day to celebrate !
Here, at the heart of this great Summit State,
Which, like a mountain-peak, exalted high,
Bathes her pure forehead in the azure sky;
Whence all the streams, as from a mountain crest, ·
Flow down to South and North, to East and West;
All ways lead downward from her upland height,
All ways lead up to her ideal site.
The Pivot State ! on which shall turn and rest
The balanced continent, when East and West
And North and South shall teem with human hands
As dense as those that toil in Asian lands;
For up to us, so Nature has decreed,
From every point the water highways lead !
The Water State ! from whose pure fountains rise
Ten thousand lakes that mirror back the skies.
Mother of Giant waters ! who gives birth
To the two Mammoth Rivers of the earth !
Grandmother of the Waters ! mighty dame !
From whom the Father of the Waters came !

Far to the North the healthy mother takes
In her clean arms the crystal streams and lakes,
And into one great river gives them form;
Then pours it southward, like a bridled storm !
Here, at our side, it thunders down the Fall,
And far-off rivers hear the mighty call,
And from a thousand miles come sweeping free,
To join the glorious march toward the sea !
And give their all to swell one river tide,
Where the vast commerce of the world may ride !

Again she takes the myriad water-skeins
Of lakes and streams from northern woods and plains,
And spins from them a sea-like tide that pours
The grandest stream that laves terrestrial shores,
Which, flowing down the world toward the East,
By rivers, lakes, and thread-like brooks increased,
Expands its tide to five stupendous lakes,
And four great rivers in its progress makes,
Till far away it leaps the world's great Fall,
And beats its way to sea at Montreal !

Here, wise men say, who look with prescient eye,
Shall the great seat of future empire lie.
Here springs the Dual City, which shall fill
The plain for miles, and cover every hill !
Playmates in childhood, hand in hand they went,
And grew and loved till their glad youth was spent.
Soon shall the nuptials come, and man and wife
Go forth one flesh to one illustrious life,

And nations see the twain to wedlock given,
And say, " Behold, a marriage made in Heaven !"

Now, while the Muse withdraws the veil, I see
The wondrous vision of what is to be;
For miles and miles along the river banks
The blocks of commerce tower in massive ranks,
A thousand domes are flashing in the sun,
A thousand streets between the structures run,
Down which I see a human ocean pour
With rush and surge and beat and stormy roar,
And far around the river wharves and slips,
Like a dead forest, rise the masts of ships;
For now, through channels made by human hand,
The seas and lakes and rivers of the land,
Are linked together, and, with flags unfurled,
The ships come up from all the busy world !

And now the scene expands beneath my eyes,
I see, far out, a mile-long depot rise,
Where, with a great and never-ceasing din,
The long-drawn trains from all the world come in !
Far to the North I see a great train glide,
And sweep across to the Pacific side,
And, turning northward, through the Polar gate,
Thrid a long tunnel under Behring's Strait;
Then shout to Asia, and go thundering down
Through many an old and many-peopled town,
And fleeing westward through a hundred States,
O'er classic streams and under tunneled straits,

Rise, screaming, from the ground on Britain's shores,
And London, sea-like, round it breaks and roars !

Around these Falls, if we believe the wise,
The world's great Capital may yet arise !
One constitution then shall join mankind,
And rights before obscure, be well defined,
And here, from year to year, in all men's cause,
The world shall meet to frame its general laws !

The day dawns now in which our sons shall view
The place we builded better than we knew;
For we shall build the City of the Free—
The heart of man's great State—which is to be.
The Capital of Men, and not of Kings,
Where Toil and Merit are the honored things,
Whose halls of learning and of art shall rise,
Free as the air, to make the many wise,
And o'er whose domes the flag shall be unfurled
Of one United States of all the World !

POEMS IN THE RELIGIOUS VEIN.

RESURRECTION.

Up comes the winter morning sun,
    And out of the North the winter breeze,
And the big pale moon away in the West,
    Is hiding behind the trees.

Dim, thin and pale, on the rim of the hills,
    It sinks away from the sight,
Like the vanishing ghost of a splendid World
    That died in the sky last night.

The winter sun is gone to his grave
    In the West, like a king that died,
And the big bright moon comes up the East,
    Redeemed and glorified.

There is no Death: nor in the grave
    Shall anything that lived remain;
And moons, and stars, and suns, and men,
    That set shall rise again !

OUR SHIPS.

In those bright summer mornings when I row
   Far out, with winds and waters sweeping free,
Among the stately boats that come and go,
   I join the toy-ships going out to sea;
Each little ship propelled by paper sails,
And given with shouts to billows and to gales !

Ah, happy boys ! that launch your ships away,
   Playing the merchant long before your time,
We men are like you to our dying day,
   Still sending ships to every distant clime.
And while to have them back we watch and yearn,
You send them forth and look for no return.

In youth our ships for rosy LOVE we sent,
   (Long since they went in those glad days of old),
Some went for Fame, and some for Power went,
   And then we sent whole fleets to bring us Gold;
And of all the ships we sent across the main,
Not one in thousands came to us again.

But I believe our ships are gone before,
   Gone to that Better Land to which we go;
There, one by one, they gather to the shore,
   Blown safely in by all the winds that blow.
And we shall find them on some Happy Day,
Moored fast, and waiting in the Golden Bay !

RETROSPECTION.

He sits by the way and weeps,
  Worn out in his search for the Truth,
Looking back at the hills and the blue mountain tops
  In the Beautiful Land of his Youth.

There is many a grave by the way,
  Where he buried his Hopes as they died,
And the suffering which came with the years
  Has humbled his heart of its pride.

The rich in their chariots roll by,
  They have acres and money in heaps,
And they laugh at the poor weary man
  Who sits by the way and weeps.

But he heeds not their scorn and neglect,
  As he thinks of the far-away goal,
And dreams that his youth may return
  In some beautiful land of the Soul.

And he sits by the way and weeps,
  Worn out in his search for the Truth,
Looking back at the hills and the blue mountain tops
  In the Beautiful Land of his Youth.

A DREAM.

I.

Alone at night I read the Atheist's creed,
And, as I read, I fell asleep and dreamed
A wondrous dream:
      Upborne upon a cloud,
And floating far through planet-peopled space,
I joined the grand procession of the worlds.
Above, below, around, the glorious stars
Moved in supernal measures to sweet sounds
Heard by the inner ear.

      And suddenly
I heard a crushing, splitting, splintering crash,
Loud as ten thousand thunder-claps, and saw
The Universe give way !   The shining worlds
Shot from their orbits !   Mad world meeting world
In hideous collision, burst and poured
Oceans of red-hot lava down the skies !

      Then ceased all sound, all light, all being ceased,
Save I, alone; in horror and dismay,
In utter silence, utter darkness left,
Down weltering alone in endless space !
And sinking, sinking, sinking, sinking down,
I called for succor with the mightiest cry
That ever broke from any human soul !

Far through the darkness, then, I saw a light
Coming toward me, and the cloud returned
Below, and bore me up and changed my dream.

II.

Again I dreamed I saw the Universe
Far floating, anchored to the throne of God;
And Space, which seems so void to outward eyes,
Was thickly peopled. All the Universe
Was one great city. Streets of golden light
Went forth to every world, and all the streets
Were thronged with shining beings, thick as motes
That float in sunbeams, who went to and fro
Among the peopled worlds to teach and help.
With joy I saw that each world was a house
In the Great City of our Father, God,
And in each house one family, guarded by
A multitude of spirits, whose delight
And constant mission was to minister.

And thereupon, that inner, radiant Love,
With which all space was palpitant and warm,
Came over me, and in a semi-swoon
Of sleep in sleep, I sank to rosy depths
Of deep and blissful rest, and dreamed no more.

COME CLOSE.

Come close, my child! the tempest rages high—
Come close to me until it passes by;
I guide the winds and lightnings by my hand—
Come close, there is no tempest where I stand.

Come close, my child! Your love is not in vain,
Though unreturned, and yielding bitter pain;
Come close to me, my child! and find, indeed,
The one true Friend and Lover whom you need.

Come close to me, my child! I know your shame;
I know what tongues are busy with your name;
I know how lone and friendless you shall be,
Come close, and find companionship in me.

Come close to me, my child! and do not weep—
Your loved ones are not dead, but taking sleep;
After their toil they need refreshing rest,
Come close, and find them sleeping on my breast.

Come close, my child! whatever may befall,
And find relief and comfort through it all;
In every trouble, and forevermore,
Come close to me, my child! and be secure!

LIFE.

A mystery to himself is man,
  His strangest thought is that he is;
Dismayed, he strives in vain to scan
  How came this awful life of his.
Whence and what are we ?   Whither tend
These lives that seem in death to end ?
Real or unreal, howe'er it seem,
God is, or there could be no dream.

Still the old search goes on, and all
  The Universe, from pole to pole,
Sprinkled with worlds, man finds too small
  To fill and satisfy the soul.
The heart grows weary of Earth's joys,
And, like a babe fatigued with toys,
Casts them aside in sighing mood,
And reaches out its hands to God.

Reaches, and finds in Duty done,
  In loving help to human kind;
Who stoops and lifts a fallen one,
  His own soul lifted up shall find.
Who clothes and feeds a brother man,
And brings warm blood to faces wan,
Shall find his own soul clothed and fed,
And Heaven dawn in him, rosy red.

But not to Bliss shall men attain
  In this harsh school of growth and strife;

Yet, having won by toil and pain,
    Who shall regret the pangs of life?
Who would regret the Past's long Night,
With all its fear and chill and blight,
If now the East, through twilight gray,
Were streaked with Everlasting Day?

God lifts the soul or casts it down,
    And schools it in His own wise way,
And fits it to receive a crown,
    In some great Coronation Day.
Hope cries, "Rejoice! thou shalt be blest!"
Faith cries, "Whate'er befall is best;
"Come, drink the sweet or bitter cup,
"And suffer on and struggle up."

HUMILIATION.

This gifted man, beloved by all who know him,
    Learned, religious, beautiful and brave,
Is yet in darkness, as the Heavens will show him,
    And bend him to the dust, but bend to save.
The Spirit dwells in him, yet by its side,
In royal state enthroned, are Self and Pride.

Therefore shall come long years of sore affliction,
    Of pain and pleading underneath the rod;
Self must be conquered ere the Benediction
    Can rest upon him from a jealous God.
Only the humble head can wear God's crown,
And Heaven, to win a soul, must bring it down!

GOD'S GARDEN.

There is a spot of holy ground
   Beyond the city lying—
A Garden, where there is a sound
   Of birds and breezes sighing.

And in that Garden, side by side,
   The beds are heaped and slanted,
And in each long and narrow bed
   A deathless seed is planted.

A thousand beds are there; the rows
   Are cut by paths asunder;
By each a stone is set, that shows
   What seed is waiting under.

And bleeding hearts through all the strife,
   Believe and hope, while praying,
That forming to immortal life,
   On earth is named decaying—

And that an Endless Day shall rise,
   And bring a Morning Hour,
When from each seed that waiting lies,
   Shall spring a iiving flower;—

A flower that shall never fade,
   From blight or winter hoary,
But grow and blossom on, arrayed
   In everlasting glory;—

That each shall be a bloom so rare,
   And with such beauty swelling,
That God shall want a flower so fair
   In his Eternal Dwelling—

And that His Holy Ones shall come,
   In that Illustrious Morning,
And plant them in a Happy Home,
   To bloom for its adorning !

ECSTASY.

Whence all this wondrous beauty in the skies ?
   And earth transformed, transfigured, born anew ?
Why, every zephyr smells of Paradise !
   And Heaven itself hangs round the mountains blue !
All my pure hopes and visions cherished long,
   All my youth's rapture, and its purpose high,
Come crowding through my heart, as a great throng
   Crowds through a street to see a Queen pass by!
I know not how was wrought this change so bright,
   But while I prayed, and deemed myself alone,
I had a sense of Presence, and a Light
   Before my dazzled eyes a moment shone !
Then all my soul with mystic love was filled,
And waves of rapture through my being thrilled !

THE RACE.

Whatever may, in Time, befall,
   Must end in love and right at last;
   To-day is better than the Past,   .
And Love must own and govern all.

This Love, while individual men
   And states go down, has set its face
   To bring perfection to the Race,
And men and states shall fall till then.

As if some world in space should grope
   And wander in a depth of Night,
   And feel the drawing of the light,
And suffer on in fear and hope,

And find at length its central sun
   And destined orbit, and foraye
   Roll onward, bathed in perfect day,
With bliss achieved and suffering done;

So gropes the Race in search of God,
   And in the darkness feels a hand;
   And yet shall reach the destined land,
And enter in some blest abode.

God sees more far than planets roll,
   Nor weary grows, nor faint at heart,
   And that to Him is but a part
Which to our sight appears the whole.

And from earth's dust and toil and strife,
    And from life's transient pains and cares,
    The Race constructs the unseen stairs,
And climbs into the perfect life.

THE DOCTOR'S MESSAGE.

My little patient, gone so soon before,
To that mysterious, much-desired shore;
When you come there, where yet I hope to be,
What will you tell our Blessed Lord for me?
Will you remember I was kind to you?
And tell Him all the good I sought to do?

Or will you tell him I am bruised and sore?
And that my heart is tender to the core?
Or will you ask Him to remove my pain,
And give my darlings back to me again?
Nay, tell him this—that I was kind to you,
And how I wrought my best to bring you through.

And then, amid the grief I cannot tell
To any man, but which He knows so well,
He may, perhaps, bestow a peaceful heart,
Until, like you, He calls me to depart.
Remember me to Him, whate'er you do,
And tell Him, dear, that I was kind to you.

HORTATUS.

Knock off the chains of Doubt, desponding Youth!
   Who cannot see or know must walk by Trust;
Our blinded souls, that yet may see the Truth,
   Are wrapped by God's own hand in clouds of living
     dust.

We feel He is, we cannot understand;
   We call and search, and call again, and weep,
Like children lost at night, until a hand
   Takes theirs, and leads them safe through forests
     wild and deep.

There is a life beyond, else life on earth
   And Hope are given a dying soul to mock;
Why freight the ship with gems of priceless worth,
   If in Oblivion's sea we strike Death's awful rock?

Life is worth living; Nature still is true;
   Through every wreck and change the soul remains;
And Love is not a fleeting sunset hue,
   Nor false and phantom isle that looms on desert
     plains.

Strive on, while struggling up the Alp of Time,
   Though rocks betray, and avalanches fall;
Such chances fill with poetry sublime
   The epic of each life—and they must come to all,

Endure, though Sorrow claim thee as her own,
　Though on thy heart her burdens ever lie;
The heavens are fairest when the clouds lie strown,
　Like snow-clad mountains far around the summer
　　sky.

Obey that inner Voice, which is God's law,
　And cultivate the peace a good deed brings;
A smiling Conscience makes a bed of straw
　Soft as the siken couch of Emperors and Kings!

DARKNESS AND DOUBT.

It was a day of darkness and of doubt,
　Like those which desperate men refuse to live,
　And, in my anguish, I could not forgive
The Fate which seemed to bring it all about.
In gloom I sat and nursed my misery still,
　With stolid face toward the pictured wall,
　When on my head, and pouring over all,
A flood of sunlight through the window fell.
I moved into the shade, and nursed my doubt,
　Till through another window fell the light;
　Then the glad thought broke on me, clear and bright,
That thus God's love would always seek me out.
　All darkness and all doubt must pass away,
　And every night that falls must end in day.

VERY GOOD.

Last night I dreamed I saw a light
    Flame up the East, as red as blood,
And on the sky, in letters bright,
    These words were written, "Very Good!"

Whatever this strange dream may mean—
    Promise of good, or omen ill,
Or idle image of the brain—
    I draw a lesson from it still.

And from the mountain-side to-day,
    Above the busy world of strife,
I see how April turns to May—
    I see all Nature wake to life.

Through blooming hills and blooming downs,
    The river rolls its silver flood,
Past the rich farms and busy towns,
    And all things utter, "Very Good!"

Good all things. Good yon clouds, snow-white,
    That topple round the endless sky,
Hills, fields and rivers, day and night,
    And good to live and love and die.

So from the mountain-side of years,
    Up which I came, and failed or won,
The places watered by my tears,
    Seem sweet as gardens in the sun.

From this calm height my way seems plain,
    And Work and Duty shall be joy,
Ripened, toned down, and purged by pain,
    No ill my purpose can destroy.

And, passion laid, henceforth I know
    Passion is strong but peace is deep—
Better the river's broad calm flow
    Than the brook's tortuous rush and leap.

To-day I seem to understand
    That pain and struggle, grief and care,
Are chisels in an Unseen Hand
    That round us into statues fair.

From folly, wisdom seems to grow;
    From weakness, strength; and rest from strife;
Peace out of war, joy out of woe,
    And out of Death at last comes Life.

How clear to-day my work appears—
    To grow a perfect man for God;
So, come what may, or smiles or tears,
    I know it must be " Very Good !

MY SELF.

My Self cried out for Happiness, and said:
" Find me a mate whom I can love and wed."

And striving thus to set my Self at rest,
And searching long, I granted the request.

Again my Self cried out to me and said:
" Bind, now, the laurel wreath about my head."

So day and night I strove to win a name,
And give my Self the royal gift of Fame.

But soon the rare and splendid gift grew old,
And then my Self cried out and asked for Gold.

And striving still to make my Self content,
I gave it Wealth when years of toil were spent.

And thus I yielded, though I knew at first
No mortal draught could quench immortal thirst.

And after many days, in sore distress,
My Self cried out again for Happiness.

And then I said, " Not all the worlds that roll
Through endless space can satisfy a soul !"

" Then give me Heaven," my Self cried in dismay,
And I, unable, answered, " Seek and pray !"

ON THE DEATH OF CHILDREN.

The poor, long-suffering child had passed to rest,
From the broad prairie homestead in the West;
The friendly farmers, drawn from far and near,
With downcast eyes stood round the little bier;
The mother hid her face, and strove in vain
To hide the sobs and moans that spoke her pain;
While the strong father, wrestling with his grief,
Shook through his stalwart bosom like a leaf;
The reverent Elder, with a solemn face
And tear-moist eyes, arose and prayed for grace,
Some grief-assuaging texts from Scripture read,
Consoled the mourning friends, and, ending, said:

The empty cradle stands in many a room,
And bleeding hearts must yearn, through years to come,
For perfect little feet that never more
Shall tread, uncertain, on an earthly floor,
Measuring the dangerous space, in baby glee,
Between the father's and the mother's knee.
No more the mother shall awake and hear
The little child-voice cooing in her ear.
And oft, as through the lonely house she goes,
Her heart shall bleed to find the empty clothes,
And cry to God, "How can the happy skies
Have any need of little hands and eyes?"
And Heaven shall send no answer to her woe,
Save, " Trust His love, and let the future show !"

Once, on an Eastern mountain, far away,
A field of green, luxuriant pasture lay,
While in the peaceful vale that spread below,
A shepherd fed his flocks, as white as snow.
Day after day he turned his longing eyes
Toward the pasture waving in the skies,
And often strove in vain to drive his flocks
Up the steep sides and o'er the rugged rocks,
'Till, on a summer morn, he took the lambs
And bore them upward from the bleating dams;
Then, looking down, he saw the mountain-side
White with the climbing flocks that, far and wide,
Scaled the rough heights they would not try before;
And soon, with joyful heart, he told them o'er,
And saw them all, beneath his careful eye,
Safe with the lambs, and feeding in the sky !

    Thus the Good Shepherd, when His all-wise love
Would lead immortal flocks to fields above,
Takes the white babes, amid beseeching cries,
And draws the yearning parents to the skies !

OLD ANN.

Old Ann is gone !   The church she clung to gave
The mite that laid her in a pauper's grave.
Once she was fair—the loveliest village maid—
And was, like all things fair and frail, betrayed.
Thus, at the dawn of womanhood, were formed,
The clouds that never broke, and never stormed;

A lasting gloom, that, with repressive strain,
Clung like a grave-cloth to her heart and brain !

Thenceforth from pain she knows no full release,
No light and cheerful mind, no certain peace;
But evermore a shadow clouds her breast,
Or when she wakes or when she sinks to rest.
The friends who ushered her through gilded doors,
With greetings warm, to richly-covered floors,
And cheered her heart around the well-spread board,
With due respect, and many a kindly word,
Now, with politeness, shun her in the street,
Or pass her by, unnoticed, when they meet,
And close their doors against her; at a breath
She shrinks together, struck by social death !
Her Christian sisters at the church refuse
To sit with her, and steal to other pews;
Even the kind pastor grows reserved and cool,
The teachers shun her in the Sabbath-school,
And the glad scholars, whom she loved to teach,
Slip from her class and pass beyond her reach.
Nay, even the children in the public way .
Show disrespect, and mock her at their play.
But if, Elisha-like, in her distress,
She turns enraged, to curse whom she should bless,
No quick-avenging bears come from the wood,
To quench their cruel sport in youthful blood !
The ruthless shopmen, when she goes to buy,
Wink back and forth, and make unkind reply;
And, sorest wound of all, the very poor,

Who thought her once an angel at the door,
Now make requests as rudely as demands,
And take her gifts with condescending hands !
Her name and influence sink to sure decay,
Nor friends alone, but kindred fall away;
In vain she toils, in vain she turns to fight,
Her ruin closes round her like the night !

Thus, old in shame and grief, but not in years,
She quit the flesh and passed to other spheres;
Shaking Earth's dust from foot and soul, she turned
Her back forever on the world she spurned.
A rudely-varnished box to burial bore
The cast-off garment once her spirit wore.
No hymns were sung, no churchly rites were read,
No throng stood round with bowed, uncovered head;
But one kind soul in sheerest pity prayed,
And then an humble, ill-clad woman, said:

Farewell, Old Ann ! Among the busy throng
One heart grows tender o'er thy dismal wrong.
Rest to thy form—a painless, endless rest !
And peace eternal be thy spirit's guest !
If clouds still shroud thee in thy new abode,
There is no Father, and no pitying God !
Perhaps thy burning prayers, unheeded here,
Are richly answered in some brighter sphere.
Perhaps thy faith not all a myth shall prove,
And we shall meet some happy morn above,
The cloud gone from thy mind, and in thine eyes
Unspeakable delight and glad surprise;

Made young again, and radiant with a light
Seen dimly here sometimes by mortal sight;
And thou shalt tell me how thy pitying Lord
Never rebuked thee by a look or word,
Nor made reproving mention of thy sin,
But smiled, and said in tender tones, " Come in !
Well done, long-suffering and beloved child,
Strong in thy love, yet easily beguiled;
I loved thee through it all, and dear shall be
The very shame that drove thee unto me !
A little while from thee I hid my face,
A little moment left thee in disgrace;
But now I take thee home, and unto me,
With everlasting kindness, gather thee.
Here shall my presence make eternal day,
Here all thy tears by love are wiped away;
The many mansions of the blest are here,
Thy own eternal home is waiting near,
And thou shalt have thy heart's desire, with peace,
And joy, and honor that shall never cease !"

POEMS OF THE WAR PERIOD.

WAR.

Down in the street there's a shuffling of feet,
    And the big guns boom on the top of the hill;
There's a clatter of swords, and a murmur of words,
    And veins are swelling with blood to spill.

And the fife and the drum through the long streets
      come,
    And the flags are let loose from window and wall,
There are loud " Hurrahs !" and the brass band plays,
    And what does it mean — this music and all ?

Why, a sound went forth from the far-off South,
    And the war-dog barked ere the morning light,
And a thrill went far through the heart of the North,
    And the men rose up like a storm in the night.

The faces of women are washed with tears,
    For the men they love are in battle array;
Oh, what can the beautiful women do ?
    What can a woman, but weep and pray ?

Why, buckle the sword to the man she loves,
    And vow to be true to him when afar,
And kiss him and bless him before he goes,
    And send him away to the war.

And the very angels shall look with surprise,
    As they lean from the ramparts above;

For there lives not a man in the scope of the skies
    That is not a hero for love !

Oh, men of the North and the South stand firm,
    'Till Treason and Traitors are undertrod;
And show to the world man is king of himself,
    And how dear is the People to God.

EQUALITY.

Toil on, ye millions, and rejoice,
    The morning star is in the sky;
Day dawns, and like the skylark's voice,
    Fall the glad tidings from on high.

Deem not your station mean, who wield
    The tools of art, or turn the sod—
All men are builders, and they build
    The Temple of the Race to God.

Some hew the stone, some build the wall,
    Some in the mine must toil below;
The finer work is not for all,
    As Raphael and Angelo.

But having done his part, his strength
    For each shall build a name and home,
And all shall come and sit at length,
    Equals beneath the splendid dome.

And ye who read the times aright,
    Can see how well the work goes on,
The red Dawn driving back the Night,
    The whole world turning to the sun.

No longer shall the favored Few
　The Many bind in iron control—
To-day the Many strike anew,
　And break the chains from wrist and soul.

Again the many strike to show
　The innate majesty of man;
The People are the heroes now,
　And have been since the world began.

O, white-hot war ! O, furnace blast !
　That burns the husk and makes men shine,
And shows what seemed but dust outcast,
　Are purest diamonds of the mine.

What need of birth or royal line ?
　These trials shall make us strong and good,
Shall tinge the Human with Divine,
　And fill all veins with noble blood.

A hut's a palace, and our own
　Is that glad age which poets sing;
A hat's a crown, a chair's a throne,
　And every man's a reigning king.

There's royalty in every soul,
　All men are regally endowed;
There's might that, when it breaks control,
　Strikes like the lightning from the cloud—

A power that makes men great and free,
　And so divine in being's scale,
That when they rise in majesty,
　Hell trembles and the Heavens pale.

THE BATTLE OF THE STORMS.

The storm-gods are going to battle,
   We can hear the low roll of the drum,
Far up, from the North and the South,
   The clouds to the conflict are come.

Great cannon from battlements boom—
   From the battlements up in the sky;
And they shake the great hills of the earth,
   And flame through regions on high.

An army of clouds in the North,
   In the South the dark lines of the foe,
And they charge up the sky with a roar,
   Like the roar of the sea in its woe.

And the earth and the heavens are filled
   With the sound of the charge and the drum,
And the forests are bending before
   The blast which they make as they come.

Lo ! they meet with a terrible shock !
   And a sharp and a startling crash
Splits the sky, like the split of a rock,
   And men reel, stricken blind by a flash.

They are met in a deadly embrace,
   They pour out their blood like the floods,
And the Earth seems to leap from its place,
   As it quakes through its mountains and woods.

A pause ! and the battle is done,
   And the sign that the war shall cease,
From the walls of the East is hung out,
   The bow and the banner of peace.

The battle is over and gone,
   We can hear the far tramp of the crowds,
And the fields and the hills and the hearts of men
   Are washed by the blood of the clouds.

Thus our war for mankind thunders on,
   And the nations turn pale at the sight;
But they see the bright banner of Freedom and Peace
   Hung out on the walls of the night.

And the Nation grows rich from its gifts,
   And the People grow strong from their pain,
And the State and the Church and the hearts of man,
   Are washed by the blood of the slain.

ON THE BAR,

All day the helpless steamboat writhed and shivered,
   Clutched in the strong grip of the treacherous bar,
All day the people sighed to be delivered,
   While mate and deck-hands worked with rope and
      spar.

Silent the poet sat among the people,
   With pleasant day-dreams smiling in his eye,
And saw the town, with tow'ring dome and steeple,
   And sleepless ferry-boats that fluttered by.

Fair rose the town, with the great stream beneath her,
  And columns of smoke uncoiling on the air,
Her church-spires swimming in the crystal ether,
  And homes and gardens smiling everywhere.

All day upon the sand-bar, down the river,
  The naked urchins ran—a goodly sight—
And plunging with exultant leap and shiver,
  Swam round and round and shouted with delight !

All day along the shallow shore, the cattle
  Stood in knee deep, or idly came and went,
Switching the fly-brush in the same old battle,
  And grinding still the cud, with looks content.

Behind the pleasant town the hills immortal
  Rose green with woods and blue with summer skies;
And far beyond, as through an open portal,
  He saw the clouds, like Heaven's own mountains,
    rise.

Saw everywhere, the wide earth's wondrous beauty,
  The busy towns, the green and fruitful land,
Saw the glad world of love and work and duty,
  And prayed the Nation might forever stand.

Saw the Great People blessed beyond all measure,
  With power and room and liberty to live:
And knew a generation's blood and treasure,
  For such a land were not too much to give.

So while the rest sang songs, or told some story,
  Complained, grew restless, moved from place to place,
He talked with God, and in a far-off glory,
  Discerned a smile upon His loving face.

THE SOLDIER'S LAST LOOK.

Looking downward from the spire, over every
    busy street,
I can hear the city throbbing, like a heart, beneath my
    feet;
Ever upward, ever downward, how the busy mortals go !
How they dart, like human shuttles, back and forth,
    and to and fro !
Ever working, working, working, to the same myste-
    rious goal,
Ever seeking, ever groping, in the blindness of the
    soul !
Feeling upward through the darkness, yearning upward
    for the light,
Like the trav'lers in the mountains, on a weird and
    moonless night.

Here, above the ancient city, here above the end-
    less strife,
Let me sit awhile, and muse on all the mystery of life.
O, to think of all our trouble, and to think of all our
    pain !
O, to be forever failing, and to try and try again !
O, to be forever climbing, and forever falling back !
And to be forever struggling with the foes that haunt
    our track !
O, the dream of human glory, as I dreamed it in my
    youth,
When the sky was full of angels and the world was full
    of truth,

And my soul reached out to grasp it, as the soul will
    reach too soon,
Like a simple-hearted infant, reaching up to grasp the
    moon !
I have looked up in the star-lit nights, and in the sum-
    mer days,
And have caught a glimpse of something brighter than
    the sun's warm rays,
And the brain has paused and staggered, and the soul
    reeled back to think
Of the joy that may await us when we break this mor-
    tal link.
I have closed my eyes to listen, and have heard strange
    noises roll,
Far away, like distant thunder, down the great deeps
    of the soul;
I have heard God's great hand working, seeming far,
    yet ever near,
Slowly changing men to angels, working surely, year
    by year.
And whatever may befall us, whatsoe'er we seem to be,
We are safe, and when He binds us, it is done to make
    us free.

    Looking downward, I remember all the pleasures
    dead and gone,
And the rosy cheeks and happy hearts ere manhood's
    noon came on —
How we heard the voices calling from the far Eternity,
Heard the far-off roar of coming years, and panted to
    be free.

I was out at early morning—through the city—on the
    hill,
When the smoke went up to heaven, and the cocks
    crew loud and shrill—
When the rising sun, like God Himself, emerged into
    the sky,
And everything that lived on earth sent up a joyful
    cry,—
When a thousand westward windows answered with a
    furnace glow,
And the little angel's trumpet on the church-spire
    seemed to blow !
I was out in every Summer night, when storms were
    in the West,
And the clouds thrust out their fiery tongues, and
    licked the mountain's crest;
I was out in every Winter night, when stars were bright
    and high,
And the wondrous lights were in the North and God
    behind the sky !
There must be eternal meaning in the beauty which
    we see,
And our subtle feelings prophesy the life that is to be.

    It is Autumn, and the far-off hills, against the sky
    unrolled,
Are blue as ocean, and the woods are dipped in red
    and gold;
All around, the fields are spotted with the shocks of
    ripened grain,

Like the tents of Northern armies camping on a South-
ern plain.
And I see the rim of Winter looming up the dreary
North,
And I hear the tramp of tempests gathering far and
marching forth !

Time of strife and blood and tempests ! I can
hear the far alarms,
And the heavy tramp of armies, booming guns and
clanging arms,
For the South is drunk with Slavery, and the North is
strong and true,
And the Nation's God has called us—there is mighty
work to do !
Man was made for sacrifices—it is written on his life—
And the wife lives for the husband, and the husband
for the wife;
And they both live for the children, and each teeming
generation
Lives for that which is to follow, and we all live for the
Nation.
Man was made for sacrifices—I must place me in the
van,
And, no matter when or where or how, so I can die for
man.

I will look my last upon you—native city—hills
afar—
Ere I bind the sword-belt round me, ere I plunge into
the war;

I will look my last upon you, though it break my heart
with pain,
And a voice within me whispers, I shall never look
again.
There are many lives to offer ere the mighty work is
done,
And the lot has fallen upon me, and I know that mine
is one !
Let it be so ! who would suffer through long years to
die at last,
And be cast out and forgotten in the ashes of the
Past ?

Come and join us, O ye legions ! from the East
and West and North,
God of Freedom ! open wide thy gates and pour thy
people forth !
Gather from the fields and cities, like the tempest-
swollen rills !
Come up from a thousand valleys, come down from a
thousand hills !
Strike, if need be, till the rivers overflow with human
blood !
Strike, if need be, till the ocean blushes with the purple flood !
Strike, to banish Human Slavery from the lists of human crime !
Strike for Man and Human Freedom throughout all
the future time !

UNKNOWN.

She walks amid the graves and weeps,
    In vain she searches for her son;
Somewhere among the dead he sleeps,
    And o'er him is the word, "Unknown!"

O, mother! not until the day,
    When God shall come to wake the dead,
Shall anything his grave betray,
    Or tell where rests his sacred head.

He sleeps like him who, safe from harm,
    God buried there in Nebo's land;
Nor all the might of Satan's arm,
    Could take his dust from Michael's hand.

O, mother! with the broken heart,
    They tell thee false who write "Unknown!"
Christ from his dead can never part,
    He knows and keeps His own.

THE DOOMED CITY.

She was a city lifted up to Heaven;
Her people were exalted, and her pride
Smelt in the nostrils of a patient God.
She scorned Democracy, and ate her bread,
Not in the sweat of her imperious brow,
But in the unpaid labor of her slaves.
And while she forged the chains for other wrists,
She scorned obedience, and conspired against

The gentlest government that ever laid
Its silken laws on men. And, haughtier grown,
She spit defiance in the Nation's face,
And plotted treason in her council chambers,
And, dragging with her the third part of Heaven,
She set rebellious cannon on her isles,
And shot the flag from Sumpter.

From that hour
The people rose up like a million giants,
And men who had been dumb, found tongues to speak!
And men who had been blind, found eyes to see !
And men who had been weak, found arms to smite !
The cities shouted to the plains to strike !
And the plains shouted to the mountains, "Strike !"
And all the mountains answered back again,
And shouted to the plains and cities, "Strike !"
Then poured the legions, like the streams in spring,
And mountains, plains and cities rang with war !

And now the city's time came. Long her pride
Vexed the Almighty, and He punished long.
Through many long and terrible months it rained
Fire and brimstone and an iron hail
On the doomed city, and by day and night
Wild shrieks and screams and noises filled the air,
And monstrous missiles, hurtling through the sky,
Burst overhead or crashed among the walls !
Yet, like the Wandering Jew, who could not die,
The city could not burn. Her people ran

Hither and thither to escape the ruin
Of crushing buildings and of falling walls.
Her commerce and her glory were departed,
And grass that was to grow in Northern cities,
Grew in her busiest streets, and when she fell,
Among the shouting hosts that thronged her streets,
Were blue-clad blacks, whom once she scourged as
    slaves.

So she whose pride exalted her to Heaven,
Has been cast down and humbled; another people
Shall throng her streets and occupy her places.
Her blocks, where human flesh and blood were sold,
Are burned to cook the Union soldiers' meat;
Her blood-hounds have been hunted down and shot,
Her slave-pens have been leveled in the dust,
And the old things shall never be again.

THE MASKED BATTERIES.

The woods are gray and all alive,
    And rank on rank the rebels swarm,
Thick as the bees swarm from the hive,
    Thick as the gray clouds in a storm.
While down the field, in grim array,
Silent and masked our batteries lay.

Column on column, and gun on gun,
    Horses and men and grape and shell,
Out in the open field and on
    They pour like demons fresh from hell !

And from their batteries, thick and hot,
Fall the iron showers of shell and shot.

All down the lines, and still as death,
  Flat on the ground our legions lay;
Biding, while each man held his breath,
  The turning moment of the day.
And Rosecrans stood, with hat in hand,
And massed the guns and waved command.

But spake not.   Then the moment came,
  And from our flashing guns outpoured
The red-hot floods of iron and flame,
  Till earth shook and the heavens roared,
With peal on peal, and flash on flash,
And shriek on shriek, and crash on crash !

Then paused, as when a tempest lulls,
  The dun smoke rose and rolled away;
Thick strewn, as when a city falls,
  Guns, horses, men in ruins lay !
And, rising like a hurricane,
Our legions swept the battle-plain !

The field is won !   Our banner floats
  O'er heroes of a hundred scars;
And from a myriad lion throats,
  The shouts of victory shake the stars !
And dead and wounded, far and wide,
Lay still, or moaning, side by side.

So swift and sure the fierce cyclone
  Spreads death and ruin o'er the land,
But from such fields as Rosecrans won,
  Fixed as eternal Alps shall stand,
A home for men of other climes,
Freedom and Peace to after times !

SHERMAN'S HOST.

"Atlanta's ours, and fairly won,"
Sherman said, when the deed was done;
And History's page and Poet's lays,
Owned one more terse, immortal phrase,
While Sherman's host and Sherman's name,
Sprang into everlasting fame !

  Brave host of home-made Western men,
From mill and plow, from desk and pen;
In every battle fought to test
The sturdy manhood of the West,
And the rash chivalry of the South,
At bayonet-point and cannon-mouth,
They, on the foremost edge of battle,
In the fierce flame and roar and rattle,
Stand out amid the lurid glory—
Stand out as stands a promontory—
And break the waves of war asunder,
Which at the nation leap and thunder.

  At stubborn Vicksburg, swooping down,
On cannon-fronted fort and town,

They leap the stream, and back again
Come sweeping like a hurricane,
Cut the doomed city from the plain,
And at the grim, death-hurling walls,
Storm on until the stronghold falls.
Then on the mountains, steep and high,
They fight the Battle in the Sky,
Above the clouds, where down they hurled
The foe from Lookout, and unfurled
The grand old banner o'er the world !
Then storming hills and rocky ledges,
And deadly mountain-gaps and ridges,
They fought the Three-Months-Battle, down
Sheer to the gates of that doomed town,
Which, opening, passed the blue-clad host,
Shouting and singing to the coast !

Glad, gala march ! the march they made !
After grim war, a light parade !
From fallen Atlanta to the sea,
Singing the anthems of the free !
Shifting their shining arms they sang
'Till Georgia's woods with freedom rang !
Lightly they drew the righteous sword
And touched the fetters, world abhorred,
When the red shackles fell apart,
From the sore limbs, and sorer heart.
Thus when Saladin tossed in air
The silken scarf, and met it there
With his keen sword, the blade passed through,

And the rare fabric fell in two !
Lightly they heard the slave-chains break,
While myriads freed fell in their wake,
Panting and following night and day,
To reach the Freeland far away !

Rome called Marcellus Sword of Rome,
So, gallant host ! in thy far home,
Men call thee Sword, as, keen and bright,
They see thee smiting, and thy light
Flashing and glimmering in the sun,
Along the fields thy edge has won !

Sword of the Union ! whose keen edge
Drives through Rebellion like a wedge,
And cuts insurgent States asunder,
While the wide world looks on in wonder;
Pierce thou the heart of Treason through !
Cut thou the Rebel Snake in two !
Divide its bones and nerves and veins,
And give its blood to streams and plains !

Henceforth, their glory, shining far,
Shall light the page of righteous war !
As in that story which is told,
In fair Italia's tongue of gold,
How a bright Angel, all unknown,
Usurped a self-proud monarch's throne,
And, journeying from the royal home,
Went up from Sicily to Rome;
And where the splendid train passed by,
A glory fell on hills and sky !

Henceforth, when history shall relate
The deeds that made her heroes great,
How Alexander conquered all,
And wept for other worlds to fall—
How Carthaginian Hannibal
First scaled the everlasting wall,
And plunging down the Roman States,
Thundered at Rome's imperial gates—
How he whom gods could scarce retard,
Napoleon, crossed the St. Bernard,
Or smote an hundred States and towns,
And plucked up thrones and plucked off crowns;
Henceforth, when her admiring pen
Recounts the deeds of hero-men,
She shall relate how Sherman's host
Cut the long passage to the coast,
Like some vast river, and went down
Through States and cities to renown.

WELCOME HOME.

O, the men who fought and bled !
O, the glad and gallant tread!
O, the bright skies overhead !
       Welcome home !
O, the brave, returning boys!
O, the overflowing joys !
And the guns and drums and noise !
       Welcome home !

Let the deep-voiced cannon roar,
Open every gate and door,
Pour out, Happy People, pour !
          Welcome home !
Bloom, O banners ! over all,
Over every roof and wall,
Float and flow, and rise and fall,
          Welcome home !

Splendid columns, moving down,
Iron vet'rans, soiled and brown,
Grim heads, fit to wear a crown,
          Welcome home !
Grim heads, which a wall have been,
Guarding sacred things within,
Facing foeward till they win,
          Welcome home !

There the women stand for hours,
With their white hands full of flowers,
Raining down the perfumed showers
          On the dear men marching home !
Do you see *him* in the line ?
Something makes him look divine,
And a glory makes him shine,
          Coming home !

Look out where the flag unfurls,
Look out through your tears and curls,
Give them welcome, happy girls,
          Welcome home !

Welcome home from war's alarms,
Welcome to a thousand charms,
Waiting lips and loving arms,
      Welcome home!

Strong man, with the serious face,
If you saw him in his place,
Marching swift to your embrace,
      Coming home,
You would weep with glad surprise!
Ah! the dear dead boy that lies
Under Southern ground and skies,
      Far from home!

Woman, with the tender eye,
Weeping while the boys go by,
Well we know what makes you cry,
      Weary home!
God be with you in your pain,
You will look and look in vain,
He will never come again,
      To his home!

And amid our joy we weep
For the noble dead who sleep
In the vale and on the steep,
      Far from home;—
For the Chief we loved so well,
For the Christ-like man who fell,
By the chosen hand of hell,
      And went home!

Take a Nation's thanks, O men !
For the Slavery Dragon slain,
And the States restored again,
　　　　Welcome home !
Limb and Tongue and Press are free,
And the People shout to see
All the glory yet to be,
　　　　Welcome home !

For the bloody work is done,
And the people shall be one,
Under all the Western sun,
　　　　Welcome home !
Man no caste nor king shall know,
White and black shall rise and grow,
And to wondrous heights shall go,
　　　　Welcome home !

MISCELLANEOUS.

MOTHER.

Away, where the Blue Ridge looks down through the
     gap,
Over mountains that slumber like planets at rest,
Where the Valley rolls outward, like Heaven's own map,
    And the Homes lie like infants asleep on its breast;—

I look from the North Mountain knob, and behold,
    O mother! the home where thy youth dreamed its
         dream,
The orchard bowed down with its apples of gold,
    The hill with the cave and the clear mountain stream.

In the days when the roses were red in her cheeks,
    And her blood, rich with love, ran as fresh as the
         rills,
When her feet were as light as the fawn's on the peaks,
    She tripped through these valleys and danced on
         these hills.

'Twas the home of her girlhood, but long, long ago,
    She went with her love to the wilds of the West,
And there in the forests Death's hand laid him low,
    And left her with only her babes at her breast.

All around her the world like a wilderness spread,
    As she staggered along with the load that she bore,

Ah! how great was her burden! and heavy as lead,
　But as precious as gold, and she loved to endure.

And she sighed as she told us the world was once bright,
　And the flowers were lovely when she was a child,
But her words fell like snow, for our young hearts were
　　light,
　And we danced as before, and we laughed till she
　　smiled.

But we learned it at last, and we learned it with tears,
　That she longed to be there with the lord of her
　　heart,
And for us she remained through the heart-broken
　years,
For we stood in the door and she could not depart.

HOMELESS.

Sitting and weeping all the day,
Seeing the ships go down the bay,
Watching the waves that climb the shore,
Climb and fall back, and nothing more.
Finding so soon that life is sad;
Finding so soon that men are bad;
Fearing to live, from self-distrust;
Fearing to die—as die he must;
Knowing that he is weak and blind;
Seeking for what he cannot find;
Waiting for that which will not come—
A heart to love him, and a home.

Sitting and weeping all the day,
Seeing the ships go down the bay,
Watching the waves that climb the shore,
Climb and fall back, and nothing more.
Symbol of what his life has been,
Climbing and falling back to sin.
Father of men ! shall his efforts be
Forever like the waves of the sea ?

HEAVEN AND HELL.

Night locks the gates of Day—the sun has passed—
  Gone down behind the mountains blue and high;
Twilight and Rest steal o'er the hills at last,
  And Angels hang the lamps out on the sky.
Across the Eastern mountains far I came,
  And deemed I should be happier by the change,
But Place will leave the anxious heart the same,
  Bliss is in state, where'er the man may range.
Sunsets and rainbows, and the skies' soft blue,
  Earth's glory, and the stars, are in the mind;
The heart must give the universe its hue—
  There is no Beauty when the Soul is blind.
We bear within us that which makes us blest,
And Heaven and Hell are carried in the breast.

IN MEMORIAM.

"Whom the gods love die young," was said,
  And most we feel the mournful truth,
Since with the still and blessed dead,
  He lay down meekly in his youth.

No more the fields and hills he loved
  With him shall laugh, with him be sad,
No more the friends with whom he moved
  Shall smile to meet him, and be glad.

We, who live on beneath the skies,
  Must wait, and walk without him now;
Nor see, above his manly eyes,
  God's signet on his royal brow.

"They do not need him there," we say,
  Who feel his worth since he is gone;
For Heaven is made of such as he,
  While here and there the earth has one.

But in the realms beyond the sun,
  His peers desired him face to face;
And prayed, that if his work were done,
  He might be with them in his place.

So, bound with us, he suffered, till
  The Angel came and set him free,
The King had some high place to fill,
  And sent the summons suddenly!

Softly his breath went as the sigh
  Of south-winds from the Isles of Rest;

Calmly he died as stars that die,
　Behind the gray hills in the West.

With Hope and Faith and Love to save,
　And happiest with his latest breath,
Who would not live his life to have
　Such beautiful and blessed death ?

Brave heart, high mind, and noble soul,
　Farewell ! until we come to thee;
Short was thy journey to the goal,
　But great thy bliss and state shall be !

THE ARMY OF TYPES.

O, a glorious fame is the fame of the fray,
　For the Banner of Stars and of Stripes !
But the mightiest soldiers of all are they
　Who march in the Army of Types !

How they come at the wave of the Captain's hand,
　How they gather with rattle and click,
And leap to the ranks at the silent command,
　On the forming-ground of the stick !

And whether it storm or whether it shine,
　And ever by day and by night,
With a click, click, click, they fall into line,
　And march away to the fight !

Each soldier moves on in his squad of a word,
　To the Drum of the Age in the van;
And armed with a two-edged invisible sword,
　That cuts through the spirit of man.

Where Ignorance sits on her shadowy thrones,
  Built round by the walls of Old Night,
They crumble and crush into powder the stones,
  And let in the Legions of Light!

Where Tyranny reigns with his foot and his yoke,
  On the neck of the poor and the just,
They cease not to smite till the fetters are broke,
  And the Tyrant is laid in the dust.

O, Army of Freedom! and Army of Light!
  O, Host of Mankind! battle on;
Till the People shall rule in their God-given right,
  And the long Night of Error is gone!

O, a glorious fame is the fame of the fray,
  For the Banner of Stars and of Stripes!
But the mightiest soldiers of all are they
  Who march in the Army of Types!

LINES WRITTEN AFTER THE FRANCO-AUSTRIAN WAR.

Is the war ended, or begun?
Was there another victory won?
  Who shall the world inform?
Perchance it was the bulging cloud,
That, big with wind and bellowing loud,
  Leads up the coming storm.

The Sphinx, Napoleon, tries his arms,
And Europe's knees knock with alarms,

The thwarted Austrians pause;
Italia gains another inch,
Nor Pope nor King her life can quench,
    Nor foes subvert her cause.

Let monarchs battle as they may,
Heaven uses tyrants every day
    To set the people free !
Behold ! the sky is all aglow,
The sun is coming up, and lo !
    The morn of Liberty !

There will be trouble long and sore,
The sea shall rise and smite the shore,
    The bolt on hill and valley fall;
The tread of nations soon shall shake
The world; men shall arise and break
    Their chains, and crush each prison wall.

The Dragon's teeth have long been sown
Throughout the nations, and anon
    The armed men shall rise;
But Liberty shall come, and then
Free men shall love their brother men,
    And earth shall be a Paradise.

King of himself, the man must reign,
Nor longer shall his prayers remain
    Unheeded and despised.
Self-rule must come, the struggling crowd,
The mass of men, are crown-endowed,
    Each man a king disguised ! ..

BROTHERHOOD.

In dreams I walked through gloomy vales,
Where barren fields and chilly gales
   The weary heart opprest;
A leaden sky hung over all,
The red sun, like a red-hot ball,
   Rolled beamless down the West.

Anon I crossed a mountain height,
And reached a land where skies were bright,
   With here and there a speck.
The blooming fields were green and red,
And clouds hung round the mountain-head,
   Like ruffles round a neck.

The glad swains at their labors sang,
With birds and bees the green woods rang,
   The plains with flocks were white;
From hills and peaks the roofs and domes
Of tow'ring fanes and happy homes,
   Shone beautiful and bright.

And azure rivers through the ranks
   Of far-off hills came broadly sweeping;
And white towns lay along their banks,
   Like flocks upon the hillsides sleeping.
Far down there was a golden bay,
   Where tides forever ebb and flow;
A city on an island lay,
   And a wilderness of ships below.

I asked what name the valley bore,
As a fair maiden ran before,
  And gathered flowers in a grove;
And, bending down her shining head,
And blushing like a rose, she said:
  "The vale of Brotherhood and Love."

O, weary men ! that walk to-day
The gloomy vale and stony way,
  Beneath the leaden skies;
The race shall cross the range between
The barren valley and the green,
  And dwell in Paradise !

O, fellow-men ! the world is wide,
Rich vales extend on every side,
  And skies are bright above;
Unite in Brother Bands as one,
And make each land beneath the sun,
  A vale of Brotherhood and Love.

THE DREAMER.

He walks among the fields, and hears
  The bees that round the blossoms hum,
While yearning for the better days,
  That never, never come.

The golden sun goes up the sky,
  The blue dome bends above;
"Dull life," he says, "that has no grief,"
  "Dull life that has no love."

"O, blue, abiding hills," he says,
  " Blue mountains in the far bright air,
" Is that the all-beauteous world I see,
  Beyond your shining summits there ?

" Too fair for speech ! but not for that,—
  " But not for that I love you so;
" Ye bring me back the dream of love,
  " That died so many years ago."

Each season as he roams the fields,
  He sighs, " the better days will come,"
And every year has less of joy,
  And every summer less of bloom.

And resting in the grass he mused:
  " God fills the future and the past,
" His Heaven is hung all round the earth,
  " And Heaven must win and rule at last.

"So let the earth roll on to-day,
  "And let the earth roll on to-morrow,
"And morning bloom and bloom again,
  "And wake the world to sorrow."

And yet he roams the fields and dreams,
  While bees around the blossoms hum,
Still yearning for the better days,
  That never, never come.

THE FLIRT.

Alas ! she's thirty-five to-day,
   And still without the love that blesses,
And here and there a snake of gray,
   Steals through the soft grass of her tresses.
Time's foot, from cheek and bosom warm,
   Has trod the pulp and hue of peaches,
And the rich blood that plumped her form,
   Is sapped away by sorrow's leeches.

Gone is the warm light from her brow,
   That flashes out when passion gushes;
Gone is the train of suitors now,
   That praised her grace and smiles and blushes.
And so the world lifts up its voice,
   Amused to think the dart reverting,
"We do not pity, but rejoice,
   She reaps the harvest sown by flirting."

Ah ! blame her not. · Through years of doubt
   And prayers for love that seemed unheeded,
The tendrils of her heart reached out,
   But never found the oak they needed.
In all the rich and wooing train
   Not one could quench her spirit's thirsting;
She never found the sun and rain,
   To ope the flower which was bursting.

O, world ! a million hearts, to-day,
   Are going down through life, and praying

For a high love still far away,
　　Forever coming and delaying.
O, hearts! that unto death from birth
　　Find not the love that should be given,
The spirits whom ye seek on earth,
　　Are waiting at the gates of Heaven !

GARIBALDI.

O, Italy ! thou poet's flame !
　　Baptized in beauty from thy birth,
　　Thou Venus of the lands of earth,
Thou hast indeed a charmed name.

Lo ! thou art free, for God is just;
　　Thou shalt make war and suffering sweet,
　　And underneath thy beauteous feet,
Shalt grind thy fetters into dust.

Lo ! thou art free! for God is just;
　　We heard thee groan, we heard thee break
　　The iron yoke from thy tender neck,
And rise up struggling from the dust.

Like one who faints, and in the strife
　　And awful struggle for his breath,
　　Fights long and fearfully with Death,
And breaks away and comes to life.

Mother of one whom not alone
　　One nation claims, but all the race
　　Looks up to with admiring face,
And says, " we claim thee as our own."

He cometh like a gathering rain—
  A tempest coming up the West,
  With thunders rolling through his breast,
And lightnings flashing through his brain,

To make thee free ! O, man from Heaven !
  Thy deeds again have taught the race
  That unto goodness, not to place
And power, the hearts of men are given.

No outward crown thy hands shall take,
  Sceptre and throne are not for thee,
  But they who make the kings must be
Superior to the kings they make.

Thy place is with eternal kings,
  Thy throne is on a race's heart,
  Thy empire never can depart,
While history lives or poet sings.

HOME-SICK.

Night in the city ! From the deep-down street
  The money-eager multitude is gone,
The watchman's club rings out along his beat,
  And the Cathedral clock, far off, strikes one.
No other sounds, save now and then huge roars
  From a great lion in his iron cage:
Perchance some memory of Numidian shores,
  Makes his heart home-sick till he roars with rage !
And deeming thus my heart goes far away,

Again among my native hills to roam;
O, lonely man ! O, lonely beast of prey !
Two fellow-exiles far away from home !
One shakes the city with protesting cries,
One only turns his face toward the wall and sighs !

ON THE HEIGHTS.

O, happy day in summer time !
    O, day all beautiful and bright !
When, hand in hand, the lovers went
    Far up the sunny mountain height.

For hours they sat and looked away
    At the vast earth and vast blue air,
And inwardly they wept to see
    That God had made the world so fair.

Below the land in billows broke,
    Or rolled a boundless sea of green,
And homes like gardens blooming lay
    With roads like garden-paths between.

Here fifty miles of river ran,
    A hundred miles of mountain there;
Woods over woods, for leagues and leagues,
    Sloped up the wide world like a stair.

The Blue Ridge reared its hundred heads
    And stretched abroad its rocky arms,
And, far along, its bulging sides
    Were spotted with a thousand farms.

Far off the summer clouds were piled,
  Like hills of snow together driven,
Huge avalanches, fallen down
  From some great Alpine range in Heaven.

All afternoon the golden gates
  Stood open in the balmy West,
And winds went up and down the earth,
  Like angels on some holy quest.

And there above the toil and strife,
  In the pure air with God on high,
They told each other all their love,
  And kissed each other in the sky !

THE WHISTLER.

He never sings, but whistles as he goes,
Nor written song nor symphony he knows,
But in those strains what music has its birth,
Into the common air of common earth !
What heavenly fountains, deep and far away,
Send up such bubbles to the light of day?
Sweet wails, as from an angel wrung with pain,
And lover's sighs from one who loves in vain,
And sparkling ripples as from mountain rills,
And far-off notes like bugles on the hills.
Some god must lie within him prisoned deep,
Who wails and murmurs in a broken sleep.
If the divine-sweet sounds he makes were caught,
And into one befitting song were wrought,
The world would laugh and weep as ne'er before,
And sing the witching song forevermore !

HOPE AND DUTY.

Who mourns because the Past is dead
  Will never win the goal of glory;
Who sees the Future rosy red,
  Will leave a name to song and story.
Who takes the Present, day by day,
  And struggles up the hills of Duty,
Will find the things for which men pray,
  Come to him in a World of Beauty !

YOUNG LOVE.

The sun has crossed the mountains high,
And swept the mist-webs from the sky,
And sipped the dews along the vales,
And fanned the earth with balmy gales,
When down along sequestered ways
A pensive, love-lorn maiden strays,
Where cool groves fringe the river side,
And gray rocks overhang the tide.

The valleys and the hills in bloom
Fill the bright morning with perfume;
From the green fields and forests come
Low murmurings, a dreamy hum;
On flower and clover-top the bee
Swings as it sips; on bush and tree
The glad birds sing; the waters pour
Over the fall with drowsy roar,
And stretching far across the globe,

Upheaved against the distant sky,
The mountains in a misty robe,
   Look down o'er clouds that wander by;
So cool and fresh their azure hue,
The maiden thirsts to drink their blue!

   Behind her, as she sat and thought
On joys and woes that love had wrought,
She heard a sound, and, with a start!
She knew the beating of a heart!
Now something like a breath she feels
As down her cheek and neck it steals,
And two strong arms her neck enclose,
While near her own a warm face glows!
She does not look—she does not speak,
For fear the blissful spell may break!
Without a word their lips have met,
Her lips with his warm lips are wet!
And Earth recedes, and Heaven is there!
Oh, mountains, hills and vales, how fair!
How all the birds and insects sing,
'Till fields and woods and valleys ring!

They took no note of time that day,
   They wandered long and gathered flowers,
She sang him many a love-sweet lay,
   And charmed away the heavenly hours.
And when the sun went down at night,
   And o'er the mountains came the moon,
They sighed to think a day so bright
   Should hasten to a close so soon.

And silently their souls communed,
    As, hand in hand, they journeyed home,
And all their thoughts, to love attuned,
    Were sweet as honey in the honey-comb.

THE PHANTOM SAWYER.

Over there the sawyer lived, over there he went
    about,
With his saw-buck and his saw, coming in and going
    out,
Until gloomy thoughts and spirits came upon him
    unaware,
And obsessed him and possessed him till they drove
    him to despair,—
Drove him desperate to the barn, in a nightmare or a
    dream,
Where the neighbors found him stark, hanging stran-
    gled from a beam.
Then they buried him apart, praying briefly for his
    soul,
Just beyond the graveyard wall, on a bleak and lonely
    knoll,
And a melancholy ghost, so the villagers declare,
From the midnight to the dawn, haunts the barnyard
    over there—
From the midnight to the dawn, still the old man
    glides about,
With his saw-buck and his saw, coming in and going
    out !

And I often lie at night, while from thought to
    thought I drift,
And I hear a phantom saw saying "Swift, swift, swift,"
Hear a sawing and a drawing, like a short and panting
    breath,
Or the heavy-labored breathing, in the closing throat
    of death.
Then a "cough, cough, cough," like a barking, croupy
    cough,
As the saw is going through, and the stick is coming off,
Narrowing down and narrowing down, to a quick and
    sudden stop,
And I hear the phantom stick, with a ghostly thudding
    drop, —
Hear a drop and hear a thud, as when a culprit meets
    his fate,
Murdered on a ghastly gallows, to appease a bloody
    State !

APOSTROPHE TO A COMET.

Ethereal Wanderer ! whence comest thou ?
    Like some great Angel journeying from on high,
Down-turning toward Earth thy radiant brow,
    And thy bright locks far streaming through the sky.
Dread visitor of old ! art come as then ?
Portending ruin to the sons of men,
Shaking dire Pestilence from thy baleful mane,
Drawing red War and Famine in thy train ?

Or does some helpful mission prompt thy flight?
   A pilot Angel sent to distant spheres,
Coming to guide dark worlds to realms of light,
   To shine and sing through countless cycle-years?
With song and music do the planets greet thee?
With smiling welcome do they run to meet thee?
Hast thou been up among the Pleiades?
Or far beyond, to brighter orbs than these?

Above all burning suns, beside some great
   And topmost star that forms a diamond crown
To the vast universe?   Didst thou relate
   That deep below the Galaxy, deep down,
It seemed upon the far frontier of space,
There was a dim and yet a lovely place,
Peopled with little forms of wondrous ken,
Dowered like the immortal gods and known as men?

Perchance thou art a Sentinel of Heaven
   Pacing thy wonted round?   Perchance from home,
From friends that love thee and from country driven,
   Thou art an Exile doomed to weep and roam?
Perchance a Shepherd in the fields of air,
Tending a flock of worlds—a glorious care!
And now art come to learn how fares the sun,
And the bright lambs that round him sport and run?

Perchance thy flight is winged from that Dread One,
   The Core of Things, the Real, the Ultimate,
The only Substance, nameless and unknown,
   Who is Existence and whose will is Fate!

To whom the boundless universe appears
A crystal bright, whose atoms are the spheres !
Perchance The Being sends thee forth to say—
Whatever lives and feels shall live foraye.

O, flaming Wanderer ! what countless eyes
 Have searched the heavens with asking, pleading gaze,
Nor answer found in all the star-sown skies !
 Canst thou the secret to the worlds emblaze ?
Then far along the stellar highways flame !
To Nature's verge the joyful yes proclaim !
Till all the stars shall shout and sing again
Their primal song, their glad creation strain !

MIDDLE AGE.

We stand upon the deck of life,
 And, looking backward, long to warn
Yon new ships coming from the rocks
 On which our keels and sides were torn.

A little to the larboard there,
 A little to the starboard here,
Will miss the rocks on which we struck,
 And bring them through the perils clear—

Till strong of will and keen of eye,
 Each one shall steer his good ship past,
Sail safely up the bay of age,
 And touch the heavenly pier at last.

WORSHIP.

She sat there in the church that summer morning,
  A beauty-nimbus round her shapely head,
While soft winds sought her through the open windows,
  From clover fields that blossomed white and red.

The green trees in the churchyard whispered gently,
  Praising her beauty to the skies above,
And all the gardens blooming out beyond her,
  Sent up in perfumed clouds their incense-love.

About the place there shone a heavenly glory,
  Brighter than her own beauty could have made,
And I believe the angels who were present,
  Were drawn around her as she sat and prayed.

And while the preacher read a text denouncing
  Worship of idols and their worshipers,
I saw the All-Beauteous in her perfect beauty,
  And in my heart bowed down and worshiped hers!

TWO BOXES.

Down at the levee, in a Southern city,
  I saw two narrow boxes side by side,
Marked with the names of two young men, and asking,
  I learned how they had died.

These two men loved one maiden from their boyhood,
  And quarreled and hated with a deadly hate;
Each swore an oath the other should not wed her,
  And, swearing, sealed his fate.

In the old days of dueling and slavery,
   When murder skulked behind the bloody code,
They met at early morning down the river,
   Along a lonely road.

Each with a friend to oversee the murder,
   They met in hate and pride,
And the code's license silencing compunction,
   They fired and fell and died.

There stark and cold they lay in narrow boxes,
   Ah, foolish well they kept their deadly
And silently they journeyed home together,
   And she bemoaned them both.

O, human hearts ! that break o'er wrongs and sorrows,
   That mourn o'er lives in folly thrown away,
When shall the earth and heavens, in love uniting,
   Bring on the Judgment Day !

OUR LIFE.

Our life is like our earth, untamed and crude,
   With vales of love-experience, bright and fair,
Jungles of self, where beasts and serpents brood,
   Mountains of deeds, high-towering in the air,
And seas of restlessness and mighty care,
   Woods of concern that intricately rise,
And sloughs of dread and caverns of despair.
   And still forever on the horizon lies
The Heaven which we seek, far in the golden skies !

AT THE PARTY.

The loveliest girls in the town were there,
 And the one above all that he loved best,
With a white rose in her night-black hair,
 And a red rose on her snow-white breast.

They sat without on the cool, green lawn,
 In the light of the moon, looking down from the
 West,
They talked of love, and he bent so low
 That he smelt the rose on her snow-white breast.

She smoothed the locks from his throbbing brow;
 And he felt so flushed and thrilled and blest,
That he leaned, with his lips and heart on fire,
 And kissed the rose on her snow-white breast.

EARTH AND SPRING.

Fled to the North the Winter King,
The amorous Earth made love to Spring;
Through March she wore a chilling frown,
And stormed and blustered up and down.

All April-time she wept and smiled,
And pouted like a testy child,
And threw some flowers on the plain,
Pouted and wept and smiled again.

In May she feigned dislike awhile,
Then burst into a glorious smile,
And, blushing, fell upon his breast,
And so the bridegroom Earth was blest.

DRIFTING.

There is a blue ocean unbound by a shore,
   On which we are drifting and drifting away,
Far o'er the expanse there are fleets of bright ships
   That we see from our deck at the close of the day.

We never can hail the bright ships that we see,
   For our shoutings are drowned in the boundless
      main,
And where are we from? and whereto are we bound?
   We are asking each other, but asking in vain.

We are launched on a limitless, endless deep,
   Far drifting and drifting, but reaching no shore,
Yet hoping forever a haven to find,
   Where fear of the tempest will haunt us no more.

Adrift on a ship without rudder or sail,
   No compass, no chart and no captain have we,
But a Power Almighty, unknown and unfound,
   Drives us and the far-shining ships that we see.

GIRL LOVE.

I cannot think nor work nor bow
   In morning prayer to Heaven above,
So full of him my heart is now,
   I cannot do a thing but love!

O, Love! thou source of bliss and bane!
   How sweetly troublesome thou art!

What pangs of bliss, what thrills of pain,
  Thou bringest to the maiden heart!

Here at the window every day
  I sit and look and wait and sigh,
To see my love come up the way,
  Like morning up the sky.

And if to me no glance is sped,
  All day I'm sad enough to die;
But if he turns his manly head,
  And lifts to me his splendid eye,—

Hush, beating heart! thou foolish thing!
  Keep back the blood, thou foolish face!
The earth seems all a downy swing,
  Swinging me up and down in space!

———

AT THE CONCERT.

Around the hall the lights shone down
On half the beauty of the town,
On swaying, perfumed multitudes,
That rustled like the summer woods;
And my own well-beloved was there,
And wore a white rose in her hair.

And while, with many a look and stir,
Men bowed and smiled their love to her,

And good-named youths whose blood ran high,
Were happy when they caught her eye,
I knew, as sure as sure could be,
She put the white rose there for me !

Ah, well-beloved ! the space is wide,
That keeps me yearning from thy side;
What hills and mountains intervene !
What seas and rivers roll between !
But Love can laugh at heights like these,
And Love can bridge the very seas !

AURORA BOREALIS.

The heavens held a jubilee last night,
　　Some festival of gods and worlds on high,
Burnished the stars to lustre doubly bright,
　　And waved their gorgeous colors round the sky.
Streamers and flags, of hues exquisite blent,
　　Quivered athwart the bright immensities,
Till all the infinite dome shone like a tent
　　Of striped silk, a-tremble in the breeze !
What great event evoked the grand display ?
　　Some high Celestial wed with heavenly bride ?
Some wandering star returned, long gone astray ?
　　Some new god called for æons to preside ?
Or was some new world launched for countless years,
And sent exulting through rejoicing spheres ?

SONG OF THE TRUTH SEEKERS.

No State nor Church that ever man conceived,
No creed of priest that ever man believed,
No past device, nor system yet to be,
Can ever make the human spirit free.
 But the Truth, the Truth, the Truth shall make us
  free,
 The Truth, the Truth, the Truth our guide shall be;
 Lead on ! lead on ! we follow wherever it leads,
 Lead on ! lead on ! above all ages and creeds,
 Lead on ! lead on ! we follow wherever it leads,
  We follow wherever it leads !

No chains nor stripes our zeal and search can stay,
The God of Nature calls and we obey,
From far within he beckons and eludes,
And shines on him who reverently intrudes.
 And the Truth, the Truth, the Truth shall make us
  free,
 The Truth, the Truth, the Truth our guide shall be;
 Lead on ! lead on ! we follow wherever it leads,
 Lead on ! lead on ! above all ages and creeds,
 Lead on ! lead on ! we follow wherever it leads,
  We follow wherever it leads !

The path we tread with martyr blood is red,
Men give us stones because we give them bread,
But every truth we find shines out afar,
No bigot power can quench the new-found star.

And the Truth, the Truth, the Truth shall make us
    free,
The Truth, the Truth, the Truth our guide shall be;
Lead on! lead on! we follow wherever it leads,
Lead on! lead on! above all ages and creeds,
Lead on! lead on! we follow wherever it leads,
    We follow wherever it leads!

Lead on! till Right the earth and heavens shall sway,
Till Wrong and Hate and War shall pass away,
Till Good alone all hearts and hands shall move,
And men shall live in Brotherhood and Love.
    O, the Truth, the Truth, the Truth shall make us
    free,
The Truth, the Truth, the Truth our guide shall be;
Lead on! lead on! we follow wherever it leads,
Lead on! lead on! above all ages and creeds,
Lead on! lead on! we follow wherever it leads,
    We follow wherever it leads!

SONG OF THE ALL-PARENT.

I am the Father and Mother in one,
Father and Mother of planet and sun,
Parent-God, Dual-God, being from whom
Issue the worlds, from my loins and my womb!

Jupiter, Saturn and Neptune and Mars,
Earth and all planets and all of my stars,

Worlds without end from my being are sprung,
And all are my schools where I nurture my young.

Jupiter, Saturn and Neptune and Mars,
Earth and all planets and all of my stars,
Rock them and roll them and swing them through
        space,
And pass them up safe to my loving embrace.

Not one can sink but it sinks to my arms,
Not one is marred but is radiant with charms,
Not one can fall but it falls upon me,
And I toss it up again, joyous and free!

All of my children shall grow into men,
Up through the spheres I shall nurse them till then,
Here in my Pleasure-Grounds ever to be,
Walking, rejoicing, abiding with me.

I am the Father and Mother in one,
Father and Mother of planet and sun,
Parent-God, Dual-God, being from whom
Issue the worlds, from my loins and my womb!